THE AUDIT COMMITTEE:
PERFORMING CORPORATE
GOVERNANCE

THE AUDIT COMMITTEE: PERFORMING CORPORATE GOVERNANCE

by

Laura F. Spira
Oxford Brookes University Business School
United Kingdom

KLUWER ACADEMIC PUBLISHERS
Boston / Dordrecht / London

Distributors for North, Central and South America:
Kluwer Academic Publishers
101 Philip Drive
Assinippi Park
Norwell, Massachusetts 02061 USA
Telephone (781) 871-6600
Fax (781) 681-9045
E-Mail <kluwer@wkap.com>

Distributors for all other countries:
Kluwer Academic Publishers Group
Distribution Centre
Post Office Box 322
3300 AH Dordrecht, THE NETHERLANDS
Telephone 31 78 6392 392
Fax 31 78 6546 474
E-Mail <services@wkap.nl>

 Electronic Services <http://www.wkap.nl>

Library of Congress Cataloging-in-Publication Data

A C.I.P. Catalogue record for this book is available
from the Library of Congress.

Printed on acid-free paper.

Printed in the United States of America

CONTENTS

1. CORPORATE GOVERNANCE AND THE AUDIT COMMITTEE 1

2. THE AUDIT COMMITTEE IN CONTEXT 9

3. A STORY ABOUT COLLECTING STORIES 33

4. NOTES ON THE THEORY OF ACTOR-NETWORKS 55

5. THE AUDIT COMMITTEE MEETING: A PRIVATE PERFORMANCE FOR A PUBLIC AUDIENCE 69

6. THE CEREMONIAL COMPONENTS OF THE AUDIT COMMITTEE MEETING 89

7. CONTENTION AND CONSENSUS 107

8. INDEPENDENCE 127

9. COMFORT 147

10. CONCLUSION 165

NOTES 177

REFERENCES 181

INDEX 191

Chapter 1
CORPORATE GOVERNANCE AND THE AUDIT COMMITTEE

'You want to know about our audit committee? Well, our deputy chairman says it's a complete waste of time because none of the members know enough about the company to make any useful contribution and they don't know what the audit committee is meant to do anyway...no, I don't agree with him...well, come to lunch and we'll tell you..'

The flurry of comment after the publication of the report of the Cadbury Committee on the Financial Aspects of Corporate Governance in 1992 suggested that research in this area might be of considerable interest. Since audit committees appeared to play a significant role in the Cadbury prescription for corporate governance improvement, I began to read about them. I accumulated a pile of relevant books, pamphlets and papers but as the pile grew, the idea of exploring it became less appealing. Much more interesting to find out about audit committees from the people who sat on them. A telephone call to a finance director friend elicited the response quoted above. The lunch was good and the contrast in views expressed about the value of audit committees was intriguing: the first ideas for this study were born.

A sub-committee of the board of directors, the audit committee is charged with matters relating to financial reporting and audit, the mechanisms through which the board is held accountable to shareholders. Structures and processes to ensure accountability have been examined in detail in corporate governance research but scant attention has been paid to the people involved in the everyday practice of corporate governance. This study explores the activities of the audit committee from the perspectives of the individuals involved, highlighting the dynamics of their relationships and offering different insights into the role which the audit committee plays.

This chapter begins by outlining the corporate governance debate which frames this study within a historical and international perspective. The audit committee is identified as an important factor within this debate, and thus as a suitable topic for research, by virtue of its role in the recommendations of the various bodies reporting on corporate governance issues. The structure of the study is described.

1.1   THE CORPORATE GOVERNANCE DEBATE

In 1776 Adam Smith wrote:
'The trade of a joint stock company is always managed by a court of directors. This court, indeed, is frequently subject, in many respects, to the control of a general court of proprietors. But the greater part of those proprietors seldom pretend to understand anything of the business of the company, and when the spirit of faction happens not to prevail among them, give themselves no trouble about it, but receive contentedly such half-yearly or yearly dividend as the directors think proper to make to them. This total exemption from trouble and from risk, beyond a limited sum, encourages many people to become adventurers in joint stock companies, who would, upon no account, hazard their fortunes in any private copartnery. Such companies, therefore, commonly draw to themselves much greater stocks than any private copartnery can boast of. The directors of such companies, however, being the managers rather of other people's money than of their own, it cannot well be expected that they should watch over it with the same anxious vigilance with which the partners in a private copartnery frequently watch over their own. Like the stewards of a rich man, they are apt to consider attention to small matters as not for their master's honour, and very easily give themselves a dispensation from having it. Negligence and profusion, therefore, must always prevail, more or less, in the management of the affairs of such a company.'(Smith, 1976:741)

Concern about the governance of corporate entities, as articulated by Adam Smith two centuries ago, remains topical today. As Deakin and Hughes (1997:1-2) observed: 'The impact of corporate decision making on interests and communities outside the firm has always been considerable. What has changed is that a large part of the political and institutional structure through which such corporate decisions were at one time mediated, has been dismantled. As a result, attention has been focused back on to the internal governance mechanisms of companies. At a fundamental level, corporate governance is concerned with the relationship between the internal governance mechanisms of corporations, and society's conception of the scope of corporate accountability.'

Definitions of corporate governance abound: accountability is a key element. Keasey and Wright (1997:2) commented: 'There is considerable debate about what actually constitutes corporate governance but its key elements concern the enhancement of corporate performance via the supervision, or monitoring, of management performance and ensuring the accountability of management to shareholders and other stakeholders.'

Pimm (1994:69) offered a more comprehensive description: 'Corporate governance is about the way businesses are run. It is about the processes by which enterprises are directed and controlled in response to the rights and wishes of shareholders and other stakeholders. Effective corporate governance therefore matters to boards of directors, to shareholders and to other parties with a legitimate interest in a company's success. Effective governance provides safeguards against both accidental and deliberate diversion of resources away from the company's objectives; it ensures that business risks are properly addressed and managed; most of all it provides the framework within which a successful business strategy can be pursued.'

The issues encompassed by this description have been brought into sharp focus by instances of financial scandal where 'the rights and wishes of shareholders and other stakeholders' are perceived to have been ignored by company management with the consequence of 'both accidental and deliberate diversion of resources away from the company's objectives'. Such instances have been cited as failures of the corporate governance framework and have fuelled the search for more appropriate structures of accountability. As Tricker (1993:2) noted: 'Today's economically advanced societies owe a great deal to a notion of the mid-nineteenth century - the concept of the joint stock, limited liability company. Elegantly simple and superbly successful, the idea of incorporating a legal business entity, separate from the owners whose liability for the corporate debts was then limited, has provided vast employment, fuelled huge economic growth and created untold wealth. But the original model of the company, in which ownership was the basis of power, no longer adequately reflects the reality of the modern corporation.'

The history of the modern corporation rests squarely on the concept of limited liability. The consequent separation of ownership from control and

3

all the associated problems of accountability have made necessary the regulatory apparatus that surrounds corporate activity. Within this apparatus, financial reporting and the audit function were developed as methods of ensuring effective stewardship[1]. The stewardship model, which underlies the UK system of financial reporting, gives primacy to the interests of owners and of creditors. The modern challenge to this model has been expressed by critics such as Kay (1996) and is clearly illustrated in the continuing debate about the objectives of financial reporting. Within a financial reporting framework designed to meet a narrower stewardship perspective, attempts to provide information relevant for decision making to an extended group of stakeholders have resulted in financial reports which appear to confuse and mislead. Despite radical proposals for reform (McMonnies, 1988), consensus on the way forward has yet to be reached (Page, 1991,1992, and Whittington, 1991, illustrate this debate).

Systems of corporate governance vary internationally, reflecting the differing cultural contexts of the development of business enterprise. However, across the world throughout the last decade, groups of business and professional leaders have assembled to discuss the issues of accountability highlighted both by financial scandal and by the rapidly changing multi-national corporate environment. Chaired by eminent and respected members of the business community - Treadway in the United States, Macdonald in Canada, Cadbury, Greenbury and Hampel in the United Kingdom, Vienot in France, Hilmer in Australia, King in South Africa - these groups have deliberated and reported. The changes proposed by these bodies focus on achieving improvements in the quality of financial reporting: they include the formation of audit committees and an increase in numbers of non-executive directors. Empirical evidence to support the value of such measures in protecting shareholders and other stakeholders is, however, limited and inconclusive. Their recommendations have met with varying responses and the examination of their effects on corporate governance practice is in its infancy. Mayer (1997:152) noted: 'Despite the intense debate, evidence on the effects of different governance systems is still sparse. Corporate governance has become a subject on which opinion has drowned fact.'

1.2   THE AUDIT COMMITTEE

This study focuses on one part of the internal governance mechanism of a company – the audit committee. Its importance has been emphasised in the recommendations of all the reporting bodies mentioned above. Following their pronouncements, audit committees have been widely established and the consequences are thus an important subject for research.

What is an audit committee? Definitions may be found in a range of reports, surveys and research studies (see, for example, Peat Marwick McLintock, 1987; Marrian, 1988; Arthur Andersen,1992; Collier, 1993; Keasey and Wright, 1993; PRONED, 1993) These definitions tend to be framed in terms of the membership and responsibilities of such a committee, from the broad: 'An audit committee is a committee of directors who are charged not with the running of the business but with overseeing how the business is controlled, reported on and conducted.' (Arthur Andersen, 1992:2) to the detailed: '..a committee of directors of a corporation whose specific responsibility is to review the annual financial statements.. The committee generally acts as a liaison between the auditor and the board of directors and its activities may include the review of the nomination of the auditors, overall scope of the audit, results of the audit, internal financial controls and financial information for publication.' (AISG, 1977, quoted in Collier, 1992:2)

Although the detail and emphasis may vary, such definitions concur that the audit committee is a board sub-committee of (predominantly) non-executive directors concerned with audit, internal control and financial reporting matters.

How does an audit committee help to improve the quality of financial reporting? The Cadbury Committee (Cadbury Committee, 1992) was unequivocal in its view of their value: 'The Committee therefore regards the appointment of properly constituted audit committees as an important step in raising standards of corporate governance.' (1992:30)

The assumptions underpinning this approach may be illustrated thus:

HIGHER STANDARDS OF CORPORATE GOVERNANCE
will be achieved by
IMPROVED FINANCIAL REPORTING QUALITY
which will be achieved by
IMPROVED AUDITOR INDEPENDENCE
which will be achieved by
AUDIT COMMITTEES COMPOSED OF INDEPENDENT NON-EXECUTIVE DIRECTORS

The report of the Cadbury Committee asserted that: 'Experience in the United States has shown that, even where audit committees might have been set up mainly to meet listing requirements, they have proved their worth and developed into essential committees of the board. Similarly, recently published research in the United Kingdom concludes that a majority of companies with audit committees are enthusiastic about their value to their businesses. They offer added assurance to the shareholders that the auditors, who act on their behalf, are in a position to safeguard their interests.' (1992:27)

Commentators in the US, however, do not necessarily share this view: '.. a corporation having an audit committee as part of its governance structure and having an effective audit committee are, of course, different matters. While there are no reliable figures available to indicate the number of audit committees that operate effectively, there is considerable anecdotal evidence that many, if not most, audit committees fall short of doing what are generally perceived as their duties. .they do not appear to be asking the hard questions or fulfilling the full range of what is expected of them.' (Sommer, 1991:91)

Similar criticism has been voiced in the UK: 'I rather suspect that, as now, the major thrust of audit discussion will take place with the finance director, chairman and chief executive, who possess a detailed and comprehensive knowledge of events. This is not a criticism of audit committee members: it is just that their perception of events and issues is, by comparison, shallow and, in reality, discussions with them will be little more than a diplomatic side-show' (Corrin, 1993:81)

Examples of problematic financial reporting have been noted even where audit committees exist (Verschoor, 1990a, 1990b) and concern about the apparent inability of audit committees to secure improvements in the quality of financial reporting in the US was expressed by the SEC Chairman Arthur Levitt in 1998, leading to the establishment of the Blue Ribbon Committee on Improving the Effectiveness of Corporate Audit Committees (Millstein, 1999)

Collier and Gregory (1996:180) commented that this debate appears to rest on assertion and anecdotal information rather than objective evidence and Collier (1996) asked a crucial question: why have so many companies established audit committees when there is so little evidence to demonstrate their effectiveness?

This study examines the gap between these views about the value of audit committees - between the formal public assertion of the Cadbury Committee about their benefits, and the scepticism expressed by commentators and those directly involved with audit committees, as indicated in the quotations noted above. The approach used recognises that such gaps may exist because of the differing understandings of those involved. These understandings are explored through the stories of audit committee activity provided by those closely involved, defined as audit committee 'participants'. Using the actor-network theory concept of 'translation', the 'micro' level of audit committee activity is explored and, through a consideration of the dynamics of the relationships within and around the committee, it is demonstrated that the audit committee performs a ceremonial role in addition to its practical operation. The intention of the study is not the derivation of further prescriptions relating to audit committee activity in the search for the ideal model, but the enrichment of existing understanding through consideration of the complex interrelationships underpinning audit committee activity, which are largely ignored in the existing literature.

In chapter 2 a review of the relevant literature demonstrates the purpose of the study in its broader context. The design, data collection and analysis process is described in chapter 3. The analytical tools of actor network theory are explained in chapter 4 and in chapters 5 and 6 the ceremonial importance of the audit committee meeting is examined, using these tools. Three concepts of importance to audit committee participants are identified within the data - consensus, independence and comfort and the links between them are explored in chapters 7 to 9. In conclusion, it is proposed that an important function of the audit committee is the generation of comfort in order to secure the legitimacy of the company within the wider community and thus gain access to resources.

Chapter 2
THE AUDIT COMMITTEE IN CONTEXT

This chapter reviews the literature on corporate governance, boards of directors and audit committees, placing this study in context. The limitations of the literature in identifying an explicit purpose for the audit committee are demonstrated: in consequence, studies which focus on audit committee effectiveness are seen to be contradictory and inconclusive. Insights offered by research into committees are also explored. The contribution of this study to the existing literature is explained.

2.1 CORPORATE GOVERNANCE: A LITERATURE REVIEW

2.1.1 An Overview of the Literature

This study focuses on the operation of a single mechanism within the corporate governance framework – the audit committee. Discussion of the broader literature on corporate governance is therefore confined to those issues which are most directly relevant to audit committee operations, and this review does not aim to be comprehensive.

Cochran and Wartick (1988) reviewed the corporate governance literature in detail but, since that date, the literature has developed extensively, and research under this broad heading may be found in a wide variety of disciplines, as illustrated by the range of journals which have devoted special issues to the subject which include Accounting and Business Research (Corporate Governance Special Issue, 91A, 1993) Managerial Auditing (vol 8, no 3, 1993), Human Relations (August 1995) and Journal of Law and Society (March 1997). Daily and Dalton have provided an annual corporate governance digest in <u>Business Horizons</u> since 1997, summarising the year's relevant research (Daily and Dalton, 2001).

Surrounding the activities of the reporting bodies mentioned in chapter 1, studies of corporate governance have been undertaken across the world, reflecting an international concern with accountability issues. International surveys such as those by Kochan and Syrett (1991) and Oxford Analytica (1992) extend our understanding but comparability, and thus the possibility of common approaches to accountability issues, remains problematic. For example, the hypothesis that the different systems of corporate governance in Germany and Japan have contributed to the industrial success of those countries in recent years has not been fully explored, although Charkham (1995) offered a detailed comparative analysis of governance systems in the UK, US, France, Germany and Japan. Some commentators have argued that, even within the broadly similar governance structures of the US, the UK and Australia, different institutional arrangements make it less likely that a remedial measure in one country will be equally effective in another (for example, Guthrie and Turnbull, 1995). This difference in approach is further underlined by the Hilmer report (Hilmer, 1993), the Australian equivalent of the reports of Cadbury Committee (1992) and the Treadway Commission (1987): Hilmer identified the primary role of the board as creating value for shareholders, a different emphasis from the focus on protection of shareholders' interests which underlies Cadbury and Treadway. This implies that prescriptions for improved corporate governance may vary in effectiveness internationally, which has important consequences for expectations about the effectiveness of audit committees, since audit committees have been adopted in the UK largely as a result of US influence.

2.1.2 Corporate Governance Theories

Issues of accountability arising from the separation of ownership from control have been discussed in the economics literature for many years[2], from the seminal work of Berle and Means (1933) through to the development of the agency model (e.g. Jensen and Meckling, 1976). While agency theory forms the dominant approach in corporate governance studies, it is not without its critics, who have challenged both its basic assumptions and its methodological approach (e.g.Donaldson,1990; Muth and Donaldson, 1998; O'Sullivan, 2000).

Keasey et al (1997)[3] outlined four views of the corporation which lead to different models of corporate governance and different prescriptions for successful governance arrangements. They summarised the agency or 'principal-agent, or finance, model' thus: 'It rests on the premise that markets...provide the most effective restraints on managerial discretion, and that the residual voting rights of shareholders should ultimately commit corporate resources to value-maximizing ends.'(1997:3) - and noted that supporters of this approach would 'tend to be suspicious of legislative changes which impose costs or obligations upon either the firms themselves or their major shareholders' although they might 'endorse the introduction of a voluntary code such as Cadbury' (1997:5). The second approach, the 'myopic market model', differs from the agency model in that it suggests that a focus on short term rather than longer term factors in the market hinders successful corporate governance and is best remedied by interventions that lead to strengthened longer term investing relationships. Shareholder 'voice' and 'loyalty' are emphasised and the possibilities of 'exit' – an important discipline under in the agency approach – should be limited. A third approach is identified as 'the abuse of executive power': those holding this perspective on the corporation argue that corporate governance can only be effective if supported by increased legislative intervention to prevent abuse such as excessive director remuneration. Finally, Keasey et al discuss the stakeholder approach which identifies the purpose of the corporation as broader than the maximization of shareholder wealth only, giving recognition to the interests of other groups of stakeholders such as employees, suppliers and customers.

Davis and Thompson (1994) challenged the agency theory approach from a political/sociological perspective, arguing that: '.. the structure of large corporations is not strictly determined by capital market pressures but results from political struggles that implicate managers and owners as well as social structures extending beyond the firm.'(1994:169). Pound (1992,1993) identified the re-emergence of a political model of corporate governance in which democratic political mechanisms have replaced the takeover and other market-based corporate controls.

Kay's trusteeship approach also offers a challenge to the agency perspective:

11

'..much of the concern with corporate governance - a concern which is largely Anglo-American - arises from the tension between the Anglo-American model and the practical reality of how large corporations operate everywhere...it is quite clear that the organic model of corporate behaviour - which gives to the corporation life independent from its shareholders or stakeholders - describes the actual behaviour of large companies and their managers far better than does the principal-agent perspective. Yet the near unanimous view of those who criticise the present structure of corporate governance is that reality should be made to conform to the model. The principal-agent structure should be made more effective, through closer shareholder involvement and supervision. All experience suggests that this is not very likely to happen, and would not improve the functioning of corporations if it did. The alternative approach - of adapting the model to reality rather than reality to the model - deserves equal consideration. After all, no one disputes that the German and Japanese models produce many successful companies.' (Kay, 1996:108) Despite these challenges, agency theory remains the most frequently deployed theoretical approach in corporate governance research.

2.1.3 Methodologies of Corporate Governance Studies

The extensive review of the literature on boards and directors by Zahra and Pearce (1989) concluded with an 'inventory' of future areas for research. They observed: 'There are countless lists of what boards should do. Yet, evidence on what boards actually do is not well documented.'(1989:326) Many studies in this area, while extending understanding of the relationships between board structure and company performance, tend to be inconclusive and usually repeat this call for further research to be done. They have focused on linking performance outcomes with factors such as board size (Pfeffer, 1972), member characteristics such as qualifications (Bilimoria and Piderit, 1994a) and gender balance (Bilimoria and Piderit, 1994b), to produce tentatively prescriptive proposals. Research methods employed have been predominantly quantitative, using survey methods or based on statistical manipulation of information culled from published financial reports. Johnson et al (1996), surveying the literature since Zahra and Pearce, made the following comments: 'A review of the corporate governance research... illustrates that there is no consensus

12

on what constitute appropriate measures of corporate financial performance...The lack of consensus on choice and operationalization of dependent variables severely limits the generalizability of governance research findings.' (1996:430) They concluded that: '.. given the heterogeneity of typical independent variables (e.g., the multiple operationalizations of board composition) and the dependent variables (any number of operationalizations of financial performance), it may be unrealistic to reasonably compare and summarize this body of work..' (1996:433)

Herzel (1990) offered a further methodological critique. Commenting on a collection of agency theory studies, he observed: 'I question the fruitfulness of an exclusively statistical approach to corporate governance research.....Despite an enormous amount of apparently sophisticated hypothesis making and skilful statistical analysis, the exciting new information in these papers is quite modest..' (1990:581-2)

'... a high degree of insight, ingenuity and skill has unearthed little really important surprising information.... supplemental close examinations of individual cases or small samples would help in understanding what is really going on.' (1990: 593)

However, descriptive and qualitative studies are rare, possibly because of access difficulties and the dominant research paradigm (Tricker,1994). Important examples are studies of US boards by Mace (1971) and Lorsch and MacIver (1989) Lorsch has argued strongly for a methodological shift. At a seminar in 1997[4], he 'emphasised the limitations of research studies that relied principally on data in the public domain as the basis for seeking relationships between variables in the governance field' and urged researchers to undertake interviews 'which give directors opportunities to discuss their experiences and beliefs in detail' and provide 'far richer insights into the reality of power in and around the board.' UK studies of boards and directors using qualitative methodologies have been undertaken by Pahl and Winkler (1974), Spencer (1983), Mangham (1986, 1988), Mangham and Pye (1991), Pettigrew (1992), Pettigrew and McNulty (1995) and most recently Pye (2001) and Stiles (2001), but this remains an approach that is rarely used.

The ongoing work since the 1970s of Tricker – one of the earliest UK writers to differentiate between the governance and the management of the corporation - has been of fundamental importance in the development of corporate governance as a specific area of academic study. Pettigrew and

McNulty (1995) noted that Tricker's 1978 observation that 'the work of the director, in and out of the boardroom, is rated as the most under-researched management topic' is 'still ringingly true in 1995.' (1995:848)

Tricker (1994,1996) argued that the three theoretical constructs he identified as underpinning corporate governance research - stewardship theory, agency theory and stakeholder theory - offer very limited insights into the practical workings of corporate governance mechanisms. Traditional stewardship theory relies on 'the belief that directors can be trusted' (1996:47) and provides the foundation for the existing regulatory and legislative framework but: 'Stewardship theory, by assuming rational and legal behaviours, ignores the dynamics of boards, inter-personal perceptions of roles and the effects of board leadership.' (1994:56) Agency theory is similarly constrained: 'Agency theory, by assuming that governance can be captured as a principal/agent relationship, ignores group interactions, corporate and ethnic cultures and the entire panoply of inter-personal relationships and power. Life at board level needs more to explain it than cause and effect relationships.' (1994:56)

Tricker suggested that stakeholder theory was born from: '..a fear at the societal level that the large, particularly multinational, corporation had become too large and powerful to be held accountable solely through the classical stewardship mode.'(1996:48) - but was no more helpful in a practical sense than the other theoretical approaches. Tricker urged that all these theoretical approaches should be re-evaluated in the light of evidence of corporate governance practice in Asia, presenting case histories designed to explore 'the reality of the governance process: that is..what governing bodies actually do.' (1996:50) While urging this approach, he observed that: 'Two particular difficulties with board level research are (i) obtaining the necessary degree of access and (ii) interpreting the data given the rich contextual milieu from which it is derived. A further challenge to publication is the frequent call for confidentiality, with much of the hard data being commercially and financially sensitive, and the softer, judgmental data interpersonally sensitive.' (1996:50)

These issues are discussed further in the context of this study in chapter 3.

2.1.4 The Practitioner Literature

Tricker's analysis demonstrates a gap between the approach of academic research and the requirements of those who are engaged in corporate governance practice – boards of directors. A second strand of corporate governance literature – the 'practitioner' literature – focuses on the provision of practical guidance and advice for directors and their advisers. It comprises manuals designed to assist directors, guidance published by organisations such as the Institute of Directors, articles in professional accountancy, finance and management journals, and advice for clients produced by professional accountancy firms (e.g. ICAEW, 1994; Deloitte and Touche, 1996; ICAEW, 1996). It is less tentative in its proposals than the academic literature but its assertions are largely based on anecdotal report and surveys deemed to reveal 'best practice', and no attempt is made to identify any theoretical framework for board operations. There is little evidence of either literature informing the other.

The literature on corporate governance is thus characterised as: being scattered in numerous disciplines, having a strongly quantitative methodological focus and split between 'academic' and 'practitioner' strands with little evidence of connection between the two.

2.2 THE AUDIT COMMITTEE LITERATURE

As a subset of the corporate governance literature discussed above, the literature on audit committees shares similar features. It too may be divided into academic and practitioner strands. It is largely based in the United States since the history of audit committees in the United States is longer than elsewhere, although audit committee studies have also been undertaken in the UK (e.g. Collier, 1992), New Zealand (e.g. Bradbury,1990; Porter and Gendall, 1998) and Malaysia (Teoh and Lim, 1996).

An important focus of this literature is "effectiveness", discussed further in section 2.3.2 below. However, without a clear understanding of purpose, discussion of effectiveness becomes meaningless. What, then, is an audit committee for? Why is it necessary to establish such a committee at all? Clearly, in jurisdictions where there is a statutory requirement for public companies to establish audit committees, legislative compliance is of prime importance. In countries such as the UK where audit committee formation is voluntary, this is a more difficult question to answer – Collier (1996) has suggested that the existence of audit committees under such circumstances is a 'curious phenomenon'. The following discussion reveals the limitations of the existing literature in regard to establishing the purpose of audit committees.

2.2.1 The Purpose of Audit Committees

Audit committee development in both the United Kingdom and the United States has been driven by concerns about the credibility of financial reporting, particularly in relation to the issue of auditor independence, but clear statements of audit committee purpose, aims or objectives, are difficult to find.

Marrian (1988), in surveying the development of audit committees in the UK, enquired into the reasons why companies had set up audit committees, observing that: 'Audit committees are generally set up as the result of one person's commitment to the idea, often because of exposure to it in another company.' (1988:4) Responses to his questions about reasons for formation included examples of specific events such as imminent financial collapse, as well as a reason not explicitly identified in later studies - the following of fashion, stimulated by articles in the professional press. Marrian noted that 'in many cases the reason [for formation] dictated the style' but did not explain the meaning of 'style' or explore this connection in any detail. He added an important caveat to his discussion: 'Due to time and budget constraints the answers received are accepted at face value for the purposes of this particular study although on occasions we were given hints that the reasons for set up were not always as clear cut as stated.' (1988:6) A more detailed survey of the state of the UK audit committee (Collier, 1992) asked respondents to rank a list of reasons for audit committee establishment and to give details of any further reasons not included in that list. Reasons were ranked in the following order (the most frequently cited items ranked highest):
1. Good corporate practice
2. Strengthens the role and effectiveness of non executive directors

3. Assists directors in discharging their statutory responsibilities as regards financial reporting
4. Preserves and enhances the independence of internal auditors
5. Assists the auditors in the reporting of serious deficiencies in the control environment or management weaknesses
6. Improves communications between the board and internal auditors
7. Improves communications between the board and external auditors
8. Increases the confidence of the public in the credibility and objectivity of financial statements
9. Assists management to discharge its responsibilities for the prevention of fraud, other irregularities and errors
10. Increases the confidence of investment analysts in the credibility and objectivity of financial statements
11. Provides a forum for arbitration between management and auditors
12. Possibility of legislative pressure

Additional motives cited by Collier's questionnaire respondents included:

- US influence (to comply with NYSE requirements or the influence of multinational group membership)
- corporate governance issues (improvements in the efficiency of board meetings, a discipline on executive directors, a forum for non-executive directors)
- auditing benefits (improvement of communication and collaboration between internal and external auditors, enhancement of standing of internal auditors, control of external auditors with regard to fee and scope of audit)
- ethical issues (provision of a forum for reviewing the content and implementation of corporate code of practice)
- support for the finance director in disputes.

Unlike Marrian, Collier made a distinction between reasons for establishment and catalysts leading to establishment. Catalysts include:

- company financial difficulties (leading to review of financial controls and pressure for change from bankers, auditors and other interested parties)
- influence from newly acquired companies
- influence from non executive directors with audit committee experience elsewhere
- general evolution of board structure.

However, Collier did not provide any information as to who completed the questionnaires in the companies surveyed and did not address the possibility of differing perceptions of reasons for establishment emanating from those holding different positions within a company.

The report of the Cadbury Committee (Cadbury Committee, 1992) provided an outline of audit committee structure and membership, terms of reference and a range of duties for the audit committee, but offered no explicit statement as to its purpose. As Ezzamel and Watson (1997) observed: '..the Cadbury Report does not spell out precisely what the new subcommittees are meant to achieve... and how, other than by simply attending meetings, the non-executives are to hold executives more accountable through these new committees. This vagueness regarding purposes and means is most obvious with respect to the audit committee.' (1997:69)

Given the nature of the recommendations, from the Cadbury perspective the audit committee would appear to represent the means by which the conformance role of the board (Tricker,1994) might be more effectively achieved: the purpose of the audit committee is thus to focus on issues of control and accountability. This view of the audit committee role is confirmed by commentators such as Demb and Neubauer (1992) who described the audit committee as 'the personification of the board's stewardship responsibility'(1992:93)

Audit committees have a longer history in the United States with greater opportunity for exploration of the reasons for their establishment. A study by Cobb (1993) found some disagreement between commentators during the 1980s on the purposes of the audit committee, although she identified four main functions: reduction of board liability, establishing a link between the external auditor and the board, the reduction of illegal activity and the prevention of fraudulent financial reporting. The Treadway report (Treadway Commisssion, 1987) firmly emphasised the primary role of the audit committee as oversight of financial reporting, giving priority to the latter two functions. Subsequent research by Spangler and Braiotta (1990) confirmed that audit committee members and those working with them shared the Treadway view of their purpose.

Pomeranz (1997) observed that: '..audit committees and their perceived role can be seen as vaguely unsuccessful, yet meritorious, endeavours to create a more level playing field for external and internal auditors vis-a -vis operating management. Few can quarrel with the objective, even if it has remained elusive.' (1997:281) Bradbury's study of audit committee formation in New Zealand (Bradbury, 1990) suggested that audit committees are established for three reasons: to increase the credibility of audited financial statements, to help boards of directors in meeting their responsibilities and to enhance auditor independence. His analysis of the extent of voluntary audit committee formation in New Zealand indicated that, in a purely voluntary environment, very few firms form audit committees - a finding which, as Bradbury noted, contradicts some US observations (1990:33) and highlights the difference between explicitly declared reasons for audit committee formation and implicit reasons which may be deduced from observation of environmental conditions and institutional arrangements. Bradbury (1990: 33) speculated that voluntary formation of audit committees in the US could be a means of 'forestalling regulation and quieting the press', unnecessary in New Zealand where 'there are no regulations or professional requirements that prescribe or recommend audit committees'. Bradbury also suggested that the low-litigation environment of New Zealand makes the use of audit committees as an insurance against potential directors' liability less likely.

Porter and Gendall (1993) discussed audit committee development in Canada, the United States, the United Kingdom, Australia and New Zealand, identifying corporate failure as the primary stimulus in their development and tracing their changing role and duties over time, concluding with a warning that too much may be expected of them, leading to 'unfulfilled expectations and in undermining confidence in audit committees.' (1993:23) Teoh and Lim (1996) also explained the establishment of audit committees in Malaysia as a response to corporate scandals. However, in considering the purpose for which audit committees are established, Bradbury's cautionary remarks on the impact of institutional arrangements which vary between countries are important, as confirmed by Guthrie and Turnbull (1995) who suggested that in Australia audit committees as currently conceived are unable to meet their objectives defined as follows: 'Although many currently believe that audit committees (ACs) were developed to protect investors...ACs, in fact, were developed to protect non-executive directors ... from being misled by management.' (1995:78) - a rather different perspective from those discussed above and a reason unlikely to be explicitly stated by survey respondents. Turnbull (1994) explained this view in more detail: 'All hierarchical management systems must condense information. It is not in the self-interest of subordinates to provide information about short-comings for which they are accountable. The result is that boards with outside directors, and even those with executive directors, are at risk of being kept in the dark. Historically, this is why outside directors developed audit committees... Investor interests are incidental to the purpose of audit committees in protecting directors as becomes evident from reading the publications of the leading audit firms on this topic.' (1994: 84) Some commentators have observed (e.g. Marrian, quoted above) that less explicit reasons for audit committee establishment may exist. Eichenseher and Shields (1985) linked the incidence of audit committee formation in the US to the appointment of leading ('Big-Eight') auditing firms, suggesting that this was a response to increased directors' liability: their study did not identify this as an explicitly articulated reason for audit committee formation but inferred it from company behaviour. The importance of implicit reasons for audit committee establishment is further emphasised by Harrison's discussion of the strategic use of board committees to enhance and maintain corporate legitimacy (Harrison, 1987).

Collier (1996) offered a detailed analysis of the rise of the audit committee in the United Kingdom, examining the literature on audit committee effectiveness and concluding that evidence of their effectiveness was very limited and certainly insufficient to support their rapid increase in popularity. He concluded: '..the widespread adoption of audit committees in the UK might well reflect no more than an attempt to avoid legislative solutions to deficiencies in corporate governance.' (1996:135) The study reported in this thesis significantly expands Collier's conclusion through an investigation of the understandings of the audit committee role of those involved in their activities.

The academic literature on audit committees is thus inconclusive on the matter of their purpose. Nevertheless, the most extensive focus in this literature is on effectiveness and how it may be achieved.

2.2.2 Audit Committee Effectiveness

Despite the apparent lack of connection between the academic and practitioner literatures, they share a prescriptive thrust. The academic literature is certainly more tentative in its conclusions, while the practitioner advice is hortatory and apparently unconcerned with the provision of detailed evidence to support assertions, but there is a distinct indication of common purpose. This centres on the use of the word 'effective'. A major concern of those writing about audit committees is to identify the characteristics of an effective audit committee in order to provide a model or models for practical emulation. However, such exemplars remain elusive, largely because of difficulties associated with understandings of the concept of 'effectiveness'.

The Hampel Committee, successor to the Cadbury Committee, observed that: 'The word 'effectiveness' has proved difficult both for directors and auditors in the context of public reporting. It can imply that controls can offer absolute assurance against misstatement or loss; in fact no system of control is proof against human error or deliberate override.' (Hampel Committee, 1998:52) - and suggested that the word 'effectiveness' should be removed from paragraph 4.5 of the Cadbury Code in consequence.

Within the 'practitioner' literature in both the US and the UK, advice is offered on terms of reference, desirable characteristics of audit committee members and practical detail relating to the timing and conduct of meetings (e.g. Lindsell, 1992). More recently, such literature has included advice on assessing effectiveness (e.g. Price Waterhouse/IIARF, 1993; ICAEW, 1997a; ICAEW, 2001). However, such material makes no reference to the academic literature and the selection of characteristics cited as contributing to effectiveness is not supported by evidence. The approach in the practitioner literature has been to present examples of best practice for emulation (ICAEW,1997a) but neither the source of such illustrations is disclosed, nor the criteria by which they may be judged 'best practice.'

The importance of effectiveness within the academic literature is emphasised by the frequency of reference to the concept in the titles of papers (e.g. Ecton and Reinstein, 1982; Spangler and Braiotta, 1990; Verschoor, 1990a, 1990b; Kalbers and Fogarty, 1993; Collier and Gregory, 1996) but an examination of these studies reveals that characteristics contributing to effectiveness are not always simple to define or operationalise and research into their impact is equivocal in its conclusions. Similar limitations were identified by Cameron (1986) in surveying studies of organisational effectiveness, in which he noted that evaluations of effectiveness are problematic with regard to arbitrary selection of criteria and confusion between determinants and indicators.

Within the academic literature, the earliest studies of audit committees were surveys identifying their existence and characteristics (eg

Mautz and Neumann, 1970; Marrian, 1988), followed by studies which attempted to identify influential characteristics of audit committees which contributed to effectiveness, defined in a variety of ways. Surveys of this literature may be found in Kalbers and Fogarty (1993), Collier (1996) and Collier and Gregory (1996): all conclude that the evidence collected on audit committee effectiveness is limited.

Doubt about audit committee effectiveness is expressed in both the practitioner and academic literatures. Birkett (1986) surveyed the history of audit committees in the US, analysing the effects of actions by the SEC, the NYSE, the AICPA[5] and Congress but noting that despite the manifest encouragement for audit committee formation by all these bodies, without clear and consistent guidelines for audit committee operations 'the goals for which these bodies support corporate audit committees may not be achieved.' (1986:123) Continuing doubts led to the establishment of the Blue Ribbon Committee on Improving the Effectiveness of Corporate Audit Committees in 1999 (Millstein, 1999)

Lindsell (1992) commented: '...it seems that the increasing incidence of audit committees has not yet brought about any significant improvement in perceptions of corporate accountability and has not restored confidence in financial reporting. While the newness of many audit committees may help to explain this, it may be that their effectiveness will not increase simply through the passage of time. More radical action by companies may be required if audit committees are to be the agent of real improvement in standards of corporate governance.' (1992:104)

The Cadbury Report itself included caveats relating to effectiveness: 'The effectiveness of audit committees will be reduced, however, if they act as a barrier between the auditors and the executive directors on the main board, or if they encourage the main board to abdicate its responsibilities in the audit area, so weakening the board's collective responsibility for reviewing and approving the financial statements. They will also fall short of their potential if they lack the understanding to deal adequately with the auditing or accounting matters that they are likely to face, if they remain under the influence of any dominant personality on the main board, or if they simply get in the way and obstruct executive management, and stifle entrepreneurial skills.' (Cadbury Committee, 1992:69)

'Audit committees will be as good as the people on them: effectiveness depends crucially on a strong, independent chairman who has the confidence of the board and of the auditors, and on the quality of the non-executive directors. Structure is also important...' (Cadbury Committee, 1992:69)

Clarke et al (1997) observed: '..the [Cadbury] code amounts to little more than a series of motherhood statements regarding the virtues directors must display and be seen to display, plus the recommendation for audit committees to be mandatory for all public companies ...... Significantly, nowhere does the code explain how the appointment of audit committees will ensure that the financial information disclosed by companies will be indicative of their wealth and progress.'(1997:239)

Although it is easier to observe instances where mismanagement and fraud have occurred despite the existence of an audit committee (Verschoor, 1990a), it is possible that the very existence of an audit committee and the chance of detailed enquiry by its members may be sufficient to deter potential mismanagement of resources or fraud. Schneider and Wilner (1990) attempted to establish the deterrent effect of audit but did not extend their study to encompass audit committees. The academic literature, while suggesting that the mere establishment of an audit committee is not a sufficient guarantee of effectively securing sound corporate governance, does not explore this further. Menon and Williams (1994) used frequency of meeting as an indicator of effectiveness. They observed that: 'The formation of an audit committee does not mean that the board actually relies on the audit committee to enhance its monitoring ability.'(1994:121) They examined this reliance by using meeting frequency and committee composition as indicators thereof: although acknowledging that meeting frequency is a crude measure of activity, they asserted that infrequent meetings are likely to indicate less effective monitoring. They concluded that: '..the tendency for many companies in our sample to maintain ACs [sic] which were structurally weak (i.e. with a low proportion of non executive directors) or inactive indicates that merely requiring ACs may not achieve the intended purpose. Although the structure of ACs can be mandated, their vigilance cannot.' (1994:138)

Kalbers and Fogarty (1993) studied audit committee effectiveness from the perspective of power. Their literature review provides a comprehensive survey of studies of audit committee effectiveness. They noted that the comparison of characteristics of organisations with audit committees and those without them 'provides limited insight for understanding audit committee effectiveness.' (1993:25) They observed that 'effectiveness is not captured adequately by conformity to procedural requirements' since this 'fails to measure the level of quality with which they are performed.'(1993:25) Kalbers and Fogarty claimed that their approach was 'more comprehensive and theory-driven'(1993:27). They defined effectiveness as 'the competency with which the audit committee carries out its specific oversight responsibilities' and used the concept of power to examine 'both the capabilities and the resolve required to perform effectively.'(1993:27) They concluded that effective audit committee performance requires power based on institutional support, actual authority and diligence – 'factors especially difficult to evaluate with any traditional means of regulation.'(1993:45)

Other characteristics of audit committee members have been considered for their influence on effective operation. Length of tenure was examined by Ecton and Reinstein (1982) who suggested that rotation of membership would achieve greater effectiveness because new committee members ask the 'best' questions (they did not define 'best'). However, Spangler and Braiotta (1990) suggested that membership continuity achieved by long tenure was necessary to develop effective audit committee operation.

The influence of the employment background of audit committee members has been explored by several writers. Kalbers and Fogarty (1993) linked knowledge of the firm or industry to the power balance in the relationship between audit committee member and chief executive officer and suggested that such knowledge can lead to an effective audit committee. Other studies have suggested that general business background and accounting knowledge are more important in assisting audit committee members to perform effectively than detailed industry knowledge (e.g. Knapp, 1987). Bilimoria and Piderit (1994b) investigated the effect of gender balance on audit committee performance. Lee and Stone (1997) provided evidence drawn from published reports to suggest a misalignment between audit committee responsibilities and members' potential capabilities that could undermine the effectiveness of audit committees. They did not define effectiveness but noted that: 'Actual audit committee effectiveness is impossible to observe externally except ex post in situations of corporate failure..' (1997:101)

Their research findings: '..indicate that publicly-disclosed experience backgrounds of audit committee members appeared to be inconsistent with disclosed responsibilities..' (1997:104) and they argued that this could lead to external misperceptions of audit committee effectiveness. Their work was extended by Dezoort (1998) who examined the effect of audit committee members' prior work experience on their oversight judgements.

Where effectiveness is defined as improved financial reporting quality, results have also been inconclusive. Cobb's 1993 study specified the purpose of audit committee formation as the reduction of fraudulent financial reporting and investigated the effects on this of a variety of audit committee characteristics including independence, tenure, private access to auditor, stock ownership and attendance at meetings, concluding that independence and tenure were the most important. Forker (1992), studying share option disclosure in a sample of UK firms reporting in 1987-88 did not find a strong association between the existence of monitoring devices, such as audit committees, and improved disclosure. However, Wild (1994,1996) investigated the impact of audit committee formation on the quality of reported accounting earnings, using a sample of US companies which established an audit committee before 1981, and concluded that audit committee formation leads to more informative reports and enhanced managerial accountability. McMullen (1996) reported tentative evidence that audit committees are associated with fewer detected and reported instances of error, irregularity and other indicators of unreliable financial reporting. Such differences in conclusion merit investigation but little comparative research has been undertaken.

Although these studies focus on important areas affecting audit committee performance, measures of effectiveness are difficult to establish and criteria tend to be confined to those factors which can be quantified. Cameron's observations (Cameron, 1986) about the confusion of determinants with indicators in discussions of effectiveness are amply illustrated by these studies. Definitions of audit committee goals are not clearly articulated: benefits and purposes are treated as synonymous. The purpose of audit committee activity is not always clearly outlined and the evaluation of effectiveness therefore rests on unstated assumptions which are not always consistent. The model of audit committee effectiveness presented within this literature is based on the identification of structural and procedural inputs with minimal analysis of their links to desired outputs. As Power commented in the context of audit: '..if one does not know what audits are for or what they produce, one does not really know whether they fail either.' (1997:30)

Under cover of this vagueness, different concepts of effectiveness are developed and influence the behaviour of audit committee participants, as subsequent chapters of this study demonstrate.

Within the audit committee literature two further developing strands may be identified. The first deals with the impact of audit committees on corporate fraud in the US context (Abbott et al, 2000; Beasley at al, 2000). The second examines the relationships among those involved with audit committees. This focuses on the interactions between the internal auditor and the audit committee (e.g. Apostolou and Strawser, 1990; Rezaee and Lander, 1993; Raghunandan and McHugh, 1994; Raghunandan et al, 2001) and also addresses the relationship between the external auditor and the audit committee (Kalbers, 1992) and that between the finance director and the external auditor (Hussey and Jack, 1995; Beattie et al, 2001). These studies enrich our understanding of how these relationships are managed but those undertaken in the US are exclusively based on data derived from published reports and questionnaire surveys. As with the general literature on corporate governance discussed above, there is a dearth of studies which explore the perceptions of those involved in audit committee activity, through the use of qualitative research methodologies. As Kalbers and Fogarty (1998) noted: '..it appears that publicly available information may be of limited use in understanding actions that exist at the core of corporate governance. Research that is limited to these sources may provide unsatisfactory closure on the key issues.'(1998:145) In the UK, Collier (1997) and Spira (1995, 1998, 1999a, 1999b) have used qualitative methods and Beattie et al (2001) have convincingly demonstrated the value of a mixed methods research approach in this area.

The literature on audit committees may therefore be characterised as largely US based, with separate academic and practitioner strands, theoretically dominated by the agency approach, methodologically quantitative/statistical, focused principally on effectiveness and variables relating to committee structure and composition which are posited to affect this.

2.3   COMMITTEES: A LIMITED LITERATURE

As well as examining existing research on boards of directors, a wider search on committees in general was undertaken, with the intention of identifying more developed theoretical frameworks relating to committee behaviour. Although the literature on management and organisational behaviour contains extensive discussion of groups and their operation, there has been very little research into the committee as a specific type of group. The major disciplinary sources proved to be those of public administration and anthropology.

Cohen and Mackenzie addressed committee effectiveness in the pages of Public Administration in the early 1950s. Cohen (1952) noted the important relationship between a session or meeting which is a 'clear-cut event', and the background to this event, which comprises the series of meetings of which it forms a part, together with the 'bodies or interests represented, the personal relationships and ambitions of participants, and the socio-economic nature of the terms of reference.' (1952:361) - a perspective which is developed in the discussion of actor network theory in chapter 4.

Within this framework, he suggested that criteria for the assessment of committee effectiveness should be linked closely to the purpose of the committee, distinguishing two types of assessment criteria - external and internal. The former assesses the effect of the committee on 'the world outside' while the latter 'evaluates a meeting by determining the effects on the participants themselves'. Cohen noted that these two types of criteria are interdependent, in that positive external effects are unlikely to be achieved unless participants individually experience the committee's activities in a positive way. He discussed various factors which may impede effective committee performance, including the compulsion to agree, receptivity to new ideas, homogeneity of members and the role of the chairman and relationships among members. Cohen suggested that, from his personal observation, committees comprising members of homogenous background tend to spend much time on 'professional and technical minutiae' whereas heterogeneous groups tend to 'ignore fine points of detail and seek agreement on broad issues in which members are not so much involved personally'. Cohen's approach is very much that of a psychologist[6] and several of his observations have subsequently been developed in research into decision-making and other group activities: for example, his description of the phases through which committees pass in developing cohesiveness has much in common with Tuckman's analysis of group development (Tuckman, 1965).

Mackenzie (1953) criticised Cohen from a pedagogical perspective.[7] In seeking an analysis of the operation of committees which could assist the

27

student of public administration, he observed that Cohen's approach was speculative and suggested that it was of limited practical use since experimental studies of committee behaviour would be extremely difficult to conduct (an observation subsequently belied by Barber, 1966, discussed below). He nevertheless attempted to develop an analytical framework to assist in the study of committees, noting that his own observations were not based on 'planned research' but limited personal experience.

Mackenzie began by framing a definition of a committee: 'A committee is a body of people meeting round a table, to take decisions for joint action on behalf of some other (generally larger) body of which it is the committee.' (1953:238)

In developing this definition he discussed at some length the appropriate size of a committee, its impact on the seating arrangement adopted and consequently on committee behaviour. He then proposed a classification of committees based on external relationships, internal structure and the form of decision which the committee is required to reach.

He observed that the external relationships of committee members may range across a spectrum, from a closely involved grouping where the committee meeting may constitute ratification of agreements reached outside the formal structure, to a committee where members may never have met previously and will not have knowledge of any common characteristics other than the task in hand. Although Mackenzie commented that most committees would normally fall within this range, he ignored the possibility that committees may develop across this spectrum over time: it seems likely that within a specific time frame, most committees will move from the situation where member relationships have yet to develop to one in which they may be developed to an extent that removes a substantial amount of interaction from the formal meeting arena. This idea of development over time is suggested by Barber (1966) and Bailey (1983), discussed below and is explored further in Spira (1998).

Mackenzie concluded by observing that each of these three areas of classification offers a continuous scale on which a particular committee may be sited but cannot be usefully refined any further in terms of developing a taxonomy of committees. Indeed, he appeared to believe that a study of committees may yield no useful insight.

However, some years later the pages of the same journal carried a detailed study by Maddick and Pritchard (1958, 1959) which focused on the importance of conventions of behaviour as well as formal rules in the operation of committees. The conventions of audit committee behaviour as described by those involved are explored in chapter 6.

Wheare (1955) studied British central government committees, classifying them by purpose into committees to advise, inquire, negotiate, legislate, administrate, scrutinise and control. His study used selected 'characters' - chairman, secretary, official, expert, layman, party man and interested party - and observed their roles in each type of committee. Wheare discussed criteria for assessing effectiveness, noting that it is a committee's job to decide and thus it is necessary to assess if the committee has made good decisions and if the committee itself is making the decisions, rather than some other group elsewhere. Wheare observed that if committees are to work effectively they must be 'wisely led and wisely fed', emphasising the role of the chairman in providing leadership and the importance of adequate, relevant and timely provision of information.

Wheare's 'layman' is of particular interest, bearing a close resemblance to the role of the non executive director: 'He is to check the excesses of bureaucratic and expert nonsense by the application of his own common sense...He must approach his committee work with an original and critical mind. He must animate or galvanise. It is difficult to get one word to describe this quality of a good layman. It is rather like saying that he must have all the virtues of the reasonable man and also all the virtues of the unreasonable woman. Indeed, some of the best laymen are women and unreasonable women at that.' (1955:23) [8]

An audit committee most closely approximates to Wheare's definition of a committee to scrutinise and control: 'They are entrusted with the task of seeing whether or how a process is being performed, and by the conduct of this task they serve to provide the means of some sort of control over the carrying out of the process.' (1955:205)

He observed: 'It is not easy to know how the usefulness of these committees may best be judged' but suggested that assessment of effectiveness could be achieved by asking: 'Do these committees do something or enable something to be done which, if they did not exist, would not or could not be done by officials..?' (1955:231)

Barber (1966) explored power relationships within committees, using data derived from twelve US boards of finance meeting under experimental conditions at Yale in 1962. He identified five 'dimensions' of committee decision making:

- calculation - the need to reduce uncertainty by the use of techniques to simplify and focus on specific information
- cultural - the extent to which committee operations are influenced by the values and perceptions of members and the variation of interpretation of these cultural factors
- personality and interpersonal power - the influence of personal relationships between members
- role - in particular, the variation in definition of the chairman's role and the variation of performance of different incumbents
- integration - the relationship between participation and reward for members

From the perspective of this study, Barber's observations with regard to integration are probably the most relevant: 'The time dimension, the stage of the committee's development, may be of key significance. The critical problem of integration may shift over time from a major emphasis on interpersonal affective relations to a major emphasis on developing specialized relations to the group's substantive tasks.'(1966:162). This approach has similarities to Bailey's analysis, discussed below. More recent studies of governmental committees in the US have centred on the exploration of decision-making processes using mathematical techniques of game theory.

The literature on committees within public administration thus offers limited insight applicable to audit committees, since the context is so specific and historically grounded. It does, however, point to themes which surface within this study as being of significance to committee operations in general, in particular the development of committee behaviour and conventions over time and the performance of roles by the individual members. Neither theme is addressed in the literature on boards or audit committees.

Bailey has written extensively about committees (Bailey, 1965, 1977, 1983), using university committees and Indian village councils as the sites for his analysis of methods of decision-making and the uses of 'reason' and 'passion' in the exercise of power through persuasion. His arguments will be examined in more detail in subsequent chapters, but his work is particularly relevant for its emphasis on the development of committees over time (echoing Barber, quoted above) and on the role of communicative devices in establishing, maintaining and developing committee relationships, factors which have not informed discussion within the existing audit committee literature. Sillince (2000) added an important perspective on committee behaviour by exploring the use of rhetorical power and rhetorical conflict in committees, developing a theoretical model that offers an insight into committee dynamics that has yet to be tested empirically.

The literature on committees is thus seen to be grounded in very specific contexts - national and local government, university administration and Indian villages - offering limited scope for broader generalisation or theoretical development. However, it offers an important sense of the individual people involved in committee activity which is missing from the other work discussed in this chapter.

2.4 SUMMARY

This review has demonstrated that the literature on corporate governance is founded on theoretical and methodological approaches which ignore the insights into the behaviour of boards of directors that might be offered by qualitative studies using a wider variety of methodologies. Writers such as Lorsch, Herzel and Pettigrew, as quoted above, have argued for development in this area. This limitation is also identified within the specific strand of corporate governance literature relating to audit committees. The dominant focus has been on the establishment of criteria which determine the effectiveness of audit committees but since the purpose of audit committees has not been explored in detail, this has proved problematic. The potential for differing and possibly conflicting concepts of effectiveness among audit committee participants has not been recognised. The very limited nature of the existing literature on committees has also been identified.

This study thus aims to contribute to the literature by extending the existing understanding of audit committee operation through the use of qualitative methods of data collection, analysis and interpretation within a theoretical framework derived from actor-network theory (explained in chapter 4). Through an exploration of the understandings of the role of the audit committee held by audit committee participants, it offers a potential answer to the question: why have audit committees become so popular when there appear to be widely divergent views on their effectiveness? - the 'curious phenomenon' identified by Collier (1996). The next chapter describes the design and implementation of the empirical investigation which forms the basis of this study.

Chapter 3
A STORY ABOUT COLLECTING STORIES

The literature review in chapter 2 identified audit committee activity as an under-researched area, demonstrated that qualitative methods have been used very little in corporate governance studies and suggested that they could offer insights not previously revealed. This chapter outlines the qualitative approach used in this study in an attempt to extend understanding of audit committees. The process of data collection and reflection thereon is initially presented in the form of a story to provide a contextual framework for the descriptive details of the project which follow. The limitations of the approach employed, with respect to data collection and data interpretation, are recognised and discussed.

3.1   A STORY

The entrance to the building is glass-fronted, imposing. A woman passes through the doors and speaks briefly to a uniformed security guard. He directs her to a receptionist, perched behind a massive desk, who hands her a form to complete and makes a telephone call. In exchange for the completed form, the woman is given a plastic badge. She sits on an uncomfortable sofa and waits.

Her first preoccupation is the plastic badge, which identifies her as a visitor to the building. A notice on the receptionist's desk warns: 'Security: identity passes must be displayed at all times'. The badge is designed with a stiff clip to attach to a jacket lapel but the woman is not wearing a jacket. The waiting area is busy: staff frequently enter and leave the building and are required to show their passes to the security guard. Most of the men wear their badges and the guard glances at them as they pass: most of the women carry their passes in a pocket or bag and produce them as they approach the guard. The woman waiting pockets her badge.

The walls of the reception area are lined with large abstract paintings. A nearby table is covered with copies of that day's broadsheet newspapers and tidily arranged literature about the organisation which is housed in the building. Apart from this, there is no indication of the name of the organisation or its activities.

A phone rings and the receptionist calls the woman's name. She is directed to the lift and, emerging on an upper floor, is greeted by a young woman who leads her into a large office, with wide windows offering an impressive view over the city. A man welcomes her and shakes her hand. She is seated at a round table and the man sits next to her. She declines the offer of coffee and produces a tape recorder and various papers. A conversation begins.

The atmosphere is one of affability, the participants smile and laugh, but there is also a sense of close concentration. The man leans forward sometimes to emphasise a point he is making: the woman nods in response. There is an occasional pause: the woman rephrases a question, the man considers his answer. The woman listens, writes intermittently and adjusts the tape. There are no interruptions. After an hour, the conversation winds down, the woman packs away the recorder and the man escorts her to the lift.

As the woman leaves the building, she pats her bag protectively: the data is captured. Much later, she finds the badge in her pocket.

What exactly has the woman taken away in her bag and in her pocket?

The plastic badge is a symbol. It gives its wearer legitimacy in the eyes of the doorkeeper and the members of the organisation, and allows the wearer access to certain organisational spaces - part of its building, office space and locations of its work, the site of many of the organisation's resources. Access is restricted to minimise the chance of damage to organisational assets. (Some organisations visited by the woman have received threats from terrorist groups who object to some part of the organisations' activities. Others are engaged in sensitive research work which must be kept secret for reasons of state security as well as commercial advantage.) The woman has gained physical access to the organisation by direct request which was swiftly granted in this case. The reasons for this interest her as such access is not always easily attained: some companies approached have declined to co-operate in the research project. (This has been expressed in a variety of ways, from a bald and unembellished note from a chairman to the regretful and detailed explanation from a financial director: the former makes clear that any future approach would be a waste of everyone's time, while the latter leaves the door open for possible future contact and implies that there might be mutual benefit to be gained.) The woman has speculated about the reasons for her unexpected success here. Her research project is topical and of interest to people in this organisation, who apparently wish to demonstrate a public concern about the issues raised – the man she has interviewed has publicly spoken and written on related subjects. Her background and training have much in common with the man she has interviewed but there are relatively few women of her age with similar qualifications - her age and gender therefore make her the object of some curiosity.

One of the organisation's assets is information, not just about products but about its working processes. This is what the woman is seeking to access, but physical access does not necessarily facilitate access to this knowledge since the gatekeepers may not have the knowledge which she seeks and/or may not wish to grant her access to that knowledge. Allowing physical access, they may appear to grant access to this knowledge, while in fact denying access through limits imposed within their conversations. So, access to the organisation, as symbolised by the badge, may not increase the woman's understanding in ways that she has planned.

She also has a tape recording of a conversation and some notes that she has made during that conversation. Later she will make more notes about the organisation and her impression of it. She is particularly interested in just one aspect of how the organisation works - the activities of a small group of people charged with a specific area of monitoring and control. But she needs to be able to set the activity of this group within the framework of the organisation in order to understand the particular need for this activity, so her general observations of the organisation are important.

What has the man told her? He has told her about how the group meets and carries out their work; he has told her who they are, when they meet, where they meet, how they conduct their meetings. He has told her his story of the group, not the group's story. Is there such a thing as the group's story? If there is not, how can the group work? The woman has spoken in the same way to other members of the group and other people associated with the group: she has their stories on tape. The stories are not complete: they are partial, anecdotal, skewed by the personal perception of the teller. The teller considers what members of the group would want the woman to hear, and what he (or, on one occasion only, she) as an individual would want the woman to hear. The woman hears through a filter of her own understanding and expectations. What do the stories mean?

The woman would like to meet the whole group together, to watch them at work, but the confidential nature of their activities means that outsiders are not permitted to observe. The woman therefore relies for insight into the group's activities on the individual accounts of members, together with formal minutes recording their meetings. Sometimes the stories match remarkably closely: different participants describe particular incidents in very similar ways and confirm common understandings and ways of thinking. At other times, the stories diverge and participants express widely differing accounts. Transcribing and analysing her data reveals patterns: the woman's descriptions of these patterns adds a further perspective on the group's activities.

The woman began by trying to assess whether the activities of the group are effective. To do this, it was necessary to determine the purpose of the group's activities. The publicly stated purpose is clear but it is not clear how it can be attained, operationalised, implemented. The woman begins to doubt that there is a direct link between the desired outcome and the activity of the group - that this public purpose is indeed unattainable. However, the group's activities do have other outcomes, revealed by the members stories. Each member's perspective on the value of the group to him/her can be explored. While asserting the effectiveness of the overt purpose of the group, members also reveal their own concerns and these become the focus of interest for the study.

The woman bases her interpretation on the individual members' stories and her own observations. The woman's analysis is yet another story about the group. Her purpose has changed: she is now trying to draw together the stories to reflect the conflicting views, tensions and negotiations that surround the activities of the group. What seemed a comparatively straightforward task of describing and assessing the effectiveness of the group's activities has now become messy, fragmented and unbalanced, and neat conclusions are impossible.

This story provides a sense of how the stories which form the basis of this study were collected, with some reflections on the process as it was undertaken. The following sections provide more detail to answer the questions: Why were stories sought? Whose stories were sought? How were the stories accessed? How are the stories to be understood? But first: an introduction to the companies and individuals who feature principally in this study. Names have been changed and company details are restricted to essential contextual details in order to preserve confidentiality.

3.2 DRAMATIS PERSONAE

Runic plc

This company has a long history - its name is a household word across the world. Its life to date may be divided into three 'ages': the first age ended with a series of critical events leading to effective collapse, the second began with a rescue enabled by a change of ownership and of structure, the third began with a further change of ownership and has seen considerable growth through acquisition and joint venture. The people I met in this company have been associated with the second and third ages only. Their stories displayed little reference to the company's earlier history: their concerns about accounting policy and its disclosure, and about internal control appear to be driven more by the nature of the company's activities and the markets in which it operates than by any lingering memory of the company's historic crisis. I interviewed the finance director, Max Tinker, the head of internal audit, Bernard Seaton, the external audit partner, Ronald Roberts, and the audit committee chair, Henry Morton. They appeared to be remarkably frank and open with me about all aspects of their relationships with the audit committee and with each other. Copies of audit committee minutes were also supplied.

Henry Morton had joined the board of Runic more than ten years previously at the invitation of the company chairman at that time: the two had met as members of the board of another company, Tiffin. Henry also chaired the audit committee of Tiffin at the time of the interview (he retired some months later). XYZ, the auditors of Tiffin, had subsequently won the tender for the audit of Runic, and Henry had a close working relationship with the audit team - the same team for both companies. The chief executive of Runic joined the board of Tiffin as a non executive director shortly after the interviews at Runic took place. Runic and Tiffin are both in the same industry sector.

Glengarry plc

This company also has a long history and its name is of significance internationally. It too has experienced a crisis - more recent than Runic, and very much in the minds of those interviewed. Since the crisis had demonstrated significant shortcomings in the company's corporate governance mechanisms, the company board is keen to be seen as conforming to the highest standards in this area. This was very strongly emphasised in their stories.

I met with the finance director, Alex Anderson, the audit committee chair, Martin Johnson, and the head of internal audit, Simon Middleton. Their stories were more guarded and carefully told than those at Runic, although Simon Middleton (who was about to take up another position within the Glengarry group) offered very revealing descriptions of meetings and thumbnail character sketches of participants. Their stories offered a strong sense of the operation of dominant personalities. With some reluctance, I was allowed to read audit committee minutes, under supervision.

Alex Anderson had previously been a partner in the company's external auditors. Martin Johnson had previously been finance director of the company, joining the board immediately after the company's crisis period and being closely involved in the 'rehabilitation' of the company.

Scrimshaw plc

Scrimshaw was in a process of transition at the time of interviews with the finance director, Chris Tracker, and the head of internal audit, Robin Dunston. The interviews were conducted at what transpired to be the end of a lengthy period during which the company had dominated its sector and the beginning of a period where the company's performance declined and it became the target of some public criticism. The company had been the industry leader for many years but had recently expanded by taking over subsidiary companies at home and abroad, while its main rival had recently been more innovative in core areas and had taken a commanding lead. The company had been the focus of press criticism because it did not fully comply with the Cadbury Code requirements, although the board's probity was in no doubt – the historical background of the company's ownership had led to a particular board structure which the directors had seen no need to change and up to this point the role of chairman and chief executive had been filled by one individual. The current incumbent was the focus of criticism related to the company's apparent decline. The non-executive directors (NEDs) had also been criticised for having very little business experience, coming from civil service, academic and NHS backgrounds. Retirement had led to recent changes and two new NEDs had been appointed – one who had been an executive director about 15 years previously and another who was recognised as a 'high flying' and particularly competent individual who chaired a very successful company in another industry sector. The external auditors had also recently changed from a long standing association with a medium sized firm to a Big Six firm. The first audit committee meeting with the new NEDs and auditors had just taken place and changes had already been instituted.

Harrier plc

Harrier plc is a smaller public company than the preceding three which, while manufacturing for and supplying other very well known companies and owning many popular brands, is not itself a well known organisation. It was formed through the entrepreneurial activity and acquisition policy initiated by a dynamic chairman who had recently (and apparently with some reluctance) handed over to a successor and had remained on the board (and audit committee) as a NED. An initial meeting with the finance director, Roy Milford, and the deputy chairman, Jeremy James, was followed by a longer interview with Roy Milford alone. He had previously been a partner in the firm which conducted the company's audit. I was allowed to read audit committee minutes under supervision. An internal audit department did not exist at the time of the interview but has subsequently been established.

Hobson plc

At Hobson plc, a major international conglomerate, a meeting was arranged through a personal introduction to the public relations director who was clearly very keen for the deputy chairman, Michael Tyler, to use an opportunity to publicise the positive aspects of a company often subject to unfavourable press comment. This proved to be a very unsatisfactory interview: Michael Tyler was distant, claimed not to understand some questions, delivered what might be called 'the party line' on corporate governance and would not be drawn on any detailed account of audit committee practice within the company. Oddly, he claimed to have been a member of the Cadbury Committee but his name does not appear in the report.[9]

Table 1: Principal characters

Runic plc	Max Tinker, finance director
	Henry Morton, audit committee chair
	Bernard Seaton, head of internal audit
	Ronald Roberts, audit partner, XYZ
Glengarry plc	Alex Anderson, finance director
	Martin Johnson, audit committee chair
	Simon Middleton, head of internal audit
Scrimshaw plc	Chris Tracker, finance director
	Robin Dunston, head of internal audit
Harrier plc	Roy Milford, finance director
	Jeremy James, deputy chairman
Hobson plc	Michael Tyler, deputy chairman
-	Bob Cunningham, non-executive director
-	Ken Palmer, audit partner

NB: These are the individuals most frequently quoted/mentioned within this study: the full list of interviewees may be found in table 2, section 3.4 below.

3.3   WHY COLLECT STORIES?

What gives a committee its existence? How do we know that it exists? Its meetings, even if private, may be seen as a public demonstration of its existence – a closed door, a distant murmur of conversation: "the committee is meeting". In this study, the doors were very firmly closed: requests to attend audit committee meetings were invariably referred to the company chairman who invariably refused.

Henry Morton, the audit committee chair at Runic, tried to explain this reluctance:

'I think I can understand him [the company chairman] not wanting that - we have very delicate issues around that table. In every audit committee a different collection of people will come to a different view on certain grey areas - if you've been at XYZ[10] you'll know your audit comment - how it's a borderline case and you have to exercise discretion, you have to be consistent and sometimes you look back and you think 'Well I made the wrong decision' and then you try and put it right as soon as you can but all you can do is exercise those sort of common sense standards - I'm sure I haven't been right all the time, far from it, and there are some issues, I look back and I think 'Why didn't I realise what was going on there?', not that anybody had hidden them but that this potential problem was there, you know, or I didn't realise the dimensions of the problem... so sometimes you can be in that situation but you are only human you know...'

This comment displays a rationale for confidentiality based on a lack of confidence, a fear of being judged to have made a bad decision by an external observer. It conjures up a picture of a group of men around a table behind closed doors, grappling seriously with 'grey areas', trying their best to 'exercise discretion' and 'be consistent' in the face of considerable difficulty: any interference in this process would clearly be detrimental to those on whose behalf this group is working. They would not feel comfortable in the presence of the interviewer, an outside observer and their comfort[11] is important to the achievement of their task. At the same time, Henry's rationale for denial of access offers comfort to the denied: the reference to common experience - '... if you've been at XYZ, you'll know your audit comment..'- partially draws the interviewer into the group on the basis of a common understanding, and the confession of human fallibility is disarming. This image of a dedicated group, working valiantly to discharge its responsibilities, forms part of the audit committee rhetoric and is explored further in the discussion of the role of consensus in chapter 7.

In discussing the denial of access to audit committee meetings, Robin Dunston, the head of internal audit at Scrimshaw, indicated that attendance at such meetings would not be helpful to the research as the jargon-laden nature of the interactions would be impenetrable to an outsider.[12]

Further evidence of a committee's existence is provided by the documentation associated with committee meetings: the agenda, information provided for members and the minutes. However, documentation relating to audit committees is normally only available to the audit committee members and participants, and to the remaining members of the board. Runic, unusually, provided copies of minutes: at Glengarry and Harrier I was allowed to examine minutes briefly under supervision. Elsewhere access was not permitted and most interviewees expressed some surprise at the thought that minutes could be of interest.

The lack of access to meetings appeared initially to be a major constraint on the study. Subsequent reflection has indicated the limits of a non-participant observational approach within a study that could not be pursued through intensive field work over a long time period: difficulties include the problem of understanding the language used (e.g. acronyms), the infrequency of meetings, changes in committee membership which fragment understanding of relationships and other subjective factors identified by Brannen (1987). However, the seeking of understanding of the role and conduct of audit committee meetings remained central to the study. Perhaps comparison of different accounts of the same meeting would offer equivalent insight?

Silverman (1993:157-8) criticised the use of the technique of triangulation because it ignores the situated character of accounts by attempting to bring them together to arrive at an ultimate 'truth'. Seeking consistency in accounts of the same meeting certainly proved elusive: for example, the apparently simple question 'Do people always sit in the same places at audit committee meetings?' elicited quite different responses from those who attended the same meetings. This is discussed in greater detail in chapter 6.

A further illustration of differing perceptions of meeting events was supplied at Runic where Bernard Seaton, the internal auditor, expressed considerable unhappiness about the activities of the audit committee in relation to his work. He complained that members did not understand what he did and took no interest in it because they had no operational understanding of the business. For him, this was exemplified by the low position of internal audit items on the audit committee agenda and lack of discussion about issues he raised. However, a reading of the audit committee minutes indicated that internal audit issues dominated the discussions. This contradiction served as an indicator to other factors surrounding Bernard's relationship with other audit committee participants and usefully illuminated other network formations[13]. This example highlights the importance of considering accounts of meetings in the context of the role and status of the interviewee (both within and outside the meeting), the length of time over which they may have attended such meetings and their relationships with other attendees. These insights would not have been apparent from meeting observation and the use of triangulation as a confirmatory device would not have focussed on the divergences and contradictions which steered analysis and interpretation in other directions.

Intuitively one would seek to understand how a committee works by observing the manifestations of its existence – its meetings and the associated documentation. However, since access to meetings proved to be impossible to negotiate and access to documentation was also very limited, the principal method of data collection for the study was therefore a series of individual interviews, supplemented by the study of documentation where available.

3.4   WHOSE STORIES?

To obtain a picture of audit committee activity, accounts were sought from individuals performing particular roles in relation to the audit committee. These people are described as 'audit committee participants' in this study. They comprise: audit committee chairmen[14], finance directors, external auditors and internal auditors.

Because of the range of experience of each interviewee, audit committee experience could be explored in a wide range of different types of company and over a lengthy time span. Respondents reflected on this experience and drew comparisons based on their varying roles and perspectives. This offered a picture of audit committee development over time as well as a sense of the wide variation of audit committee practice.[15] The complete schedule of interviews is shown in table 2 below.

Access to these people on an individual basis proved less problematic than access to meetings, although the sample could best be described as 'opportunistic' since it was anticipated that access would not be easy. A target list of companies was prepared where access could be assured through personal contact. Direct approaches were also made to individuals who had spoken or written publicly about audit committees and other corporate governance issues. Several interviewees offered to provide further introductions elsewhere. It is difficult to decline to follow up such introductions (particularly if calls are made during the interview!) and the number of interviews undertaken could have been extended considerably if all such contacts had been pursued. However, this would have been impractical in terms of completing the study within an appropriate time period: in addition, ongoing data analysis suggested that little benefit in terms of further insight would be gained from a larger sample within the same group i.e. large UK public limited companies. Further contextual understanding was afforded by attendance at three practitioner meetings where corporate governance issues were discussed: one was a commercially organised conference/workshop on the implementation of the Cadbury Code, another was a conference on corporate governance issues organised by the Fabian Society and a third was a discussion on audit committees organised by the Board for Chartered Accountants in Business (BCAB) of the Institute of Chartered Accountants in England and Wales (ICAEW). These occasions also offered the opportunity to contact further participants.

Table 2 gives full details of all interviews undertaken. Between February 1994 and October 1996, 21 respondents were interviewed. 12 were associated with 5 companies as indicated; the remaining 9 had no specific company connection at the time of the interviews but had broad ranging experience of audit committee participant roles. Respondents gave accounts of audit committee participant experiences at a further 29 different companies mentioned individually during interviews (column 4). All audit committee chairs were non executive directors (NEDs). All NEDs were audit committee members. The specific job titles of individuals sometimes varied between companies but discussion of duties – both in relation to audit committee activities and more generally - confirmed that roles were equivalent. The corporate governance manager was employed by an institutional investor to liaise with companies in which investments were held.

The external auditor interviewed in each case was the engagement partner. The hierarchical status within the accountancy firms involved was described thus: 'I am the group engagement partner .. we have two group partners - one's the lead partner, the senior partner with grey hair and then there's the engagement partner who runs the group which is my role..' (Ronald Roberts, XYZ)

'....if you're a [engagement] partner, you have to come [to the audit committee meeting]. You can't come on your own because you know nothing so the senior manager has to come...and the senior partner, who has no role at all unless he came, has to come too...I believe it's not enough, because the person who actually knows what goes on is the manager on the spot and she doesn't come..'(Roy Milford, Harrier plc)

These comments indicate the possibility that some members of the external auditor group present at audit committee meetings may attend in a purely symbolic status: symbolic and ceremonial aspects of audit committee activity are discussed further in chapters 5 and 6.

Table 2: Schedule of Interviews Undertaken

Company	Main role of interviewee + initials	Other audit committee roles experienced	No. of other companies referred to in interview
Runic	Finance director, MT	Audit committee chair	2
	Audit committee chair, HM	Finance director	6
	External auditor, RR		1
	Internal auditor, RS		
Glengarry	Finance director, AA	External auditor (same company)	1
	Audit committee chair, MJ	Finance director (same company)	6
	Internal auditor, SM		
Scrimshaw	Finance director, CT		1
	Internal auditor, RD		
Harrier	Finance director, RM	External auditor (same company)	2
	Deputy chairman of company		
Hobson	NED, MT	Audit committee chair	2
Various companies	NED	Audit committee chair	4
	NED	Audit committee chair	4
	External auditor		
	External auditor		
	External auditor		
	Corporate governance manager	External auditor	
	University audit committee member		
	Internal auditor		
	Company chairman		

Access appeared to be facilitated by three main factors: the timing of the study, the opportunity for a public relations exercise (although all participants were assured of confidentiality) and curiosity about the researcher.

At the commencement of the study corporate governance issues were of considerable importance to those preparing company accounts, in the wake of the publication of the report of the Cadbury Committee. There was much public discussion and many large companies (including some covered by the study) were keen to demonstrate that they welcomed Cadbury and were already at the 'leading edge' of developments in this area. The subsequent publication of the less popular Greenbury report (Greenbury,1995) on directors' remuneration appeared to dampen this initial enthusiasm to discuss corporate governance issues. The fortuitously advantageous timing of the interview programme and the value of personal introductions were emphasised by a subsequent unsuccessful attempt to establish contact with six companies identified as the leaders in reporting on corporate governance issues in a report on corporate governance disclosure in FT-SE 100 companies published by Deloitte and Touche (Jones,1996) An approach was made to the chairmen of these companies. Two did not respond at all. Two responded that company policy was to refuse access to all such approaches (one of these was a very curt note from the chairman, while the other was a much longer and apologetic letter from the company secretary, accompanied by a copy of the most recent annual report). One responded, through the finance director, that the study sounded very interesting and that the company would have been very happy to help but was currently engaged in a demerger process which made it impossible for his department to take on any other commitments. The final response regretfully informed me that the company was assisting in three other similar studies at present and was thus fully committed.

Issues of access in the study of elite groups have been discussed with specific reference to boards of directors by Winkler (1987), Brannen (1987) and Stiles (2001). Winkler described the background to a study of company directors (Pahl and Winkler, 1974) where observational methods were used and the negotiation of access took a full year with a refusal rate of over 85 per cent. Winkler commented on the paucity of studies of what directors do and, while acknowledging the obvious difficulties in gaining access, argued that 'the observation of elites in action is both technically feasible and substantially valuable' (1974:146): the importance of such observational studies lies in the contrast that is revealed with prevailing ideologies about the behaviour of directors. Brannen's observational study was based on attendance at board meetings and his account stressed the inherent problems of observing such meetings: 'While observation of what

47

was said and done was not too difficult, there was rather more difficulty in understanding the ethos of the boardroom, the degree of formality and the basis of the formality, the degree of ritual and the basis of ritual.' (Brannen,1987:172). Stiles (2001) used questionnaires and secondary and archival data, employing between-method triangulation to support data derived from open-ended interviews. These accounts emphasise the problems of researching elite groups even after access has been negotiated.

In this study, each interviewee was sent an introductory letter before the interview, explaining the project and introducing the researcher. Conversation before and after interviews indicated in several cases that curiosity about the researcher had been of some influence in the interviewee's decision to participate in the study. I qualified as a chartered accountant at a time when women entrants to the profession were still unusual: interviewees who shared my age, education and training profile were interested in my subsequent career pattern and, although my gender makes me unusual within this context, I was treated as by most interviewees as 'one of them'. This was demonstrated in assumptions made about my understanding of technical issues discussed, of the ways in which accountancy firms operate and the general business environment in which interviewees operated. In some instances, these assumptions were unfounded and I had to ask apparently naïve questions or undertake some subsequent research to fill in gaps in my knowledge. Issues relating to the role and status of the female researcher in elite studies in regard to the experience of interviewing have been discussed by Neal (1995) in the context of educational research and by Puwar (1997) in a study of women MPs. Spencer, in her study of NEDs, described being treated as a 'reasonably unintelligent schoolgirl doing a project' (Spencer, 1983:10). However, in this study, age and status differentials between researcher and interviewees were not wide and the gender difference was an apparent advantage in gaining access.

3. 5   HOW WERE STORIES ACCESSED?

Before each interview, the respondent was asked to complete and return a questionnaire, designed to capture some basic data about the respondent and the audit committee concerned, as well as to explore the respondent's views on the role of the audit committee. Following the emphasis in the audit committee literature, the questionnaire focused on respondents' understandings of the characteristics that make audit committees effective: respondents were asked to rank characteristics derived from Collier (1992).To reflect different respondent roles, questionnaires differed slightly between categories of respondent. Responses were then used as the basis of discussion in the formal interview. The questionnaires were not designed as formal survey instruments and the data has not been statistically analysed: it has been used to amplify understandings obtained from the analysis of the data collected in the subsequent interviews.

Six interviewees returned the questionnaires as requested, a further four completed the questionnaire during the interview while the remainder chose not to complete the questionnaire at all. However, in every interview the questionnaire formed the initial focus of discussion. The questionnaires that had been completed prior to interview were heavily annotated. In particular, the questions involving ranking of characteristics aroused considerable comment such as: 'These are very fine judgements: on another occasion I could rank them very differently.' (Max Tinker, Runic)

'I don't think that these can be ranked – almost all are essential.' (Michael Tyler, Hobson)

'I find these rankings pointless. Clearly they are all important but I would not guarantee that I would make the same order of ranking on consecutive days!' (Henry Morton, Runic)

All interviewees were eager to expand on their answers to the questionnaire, offering anecdotes from their experience to contextualise their answers. This emphasises the usefulness of a qualitative approach in amplifying surveys, such as that conducted by Collier (1992), by highlighting the complexities which lie behind questionnaire responses (see Beattie et al, 2001, for further discussion of mixed research methods.)

Interviews were tape recorded. Notes were made before, during and immediately after all interviews - a record of observations about the interview site and its conduct, to provide a context for subsequent interpretation. A diary was also kept in which initial impressions of the interview and interviewee were recorded, together with tentative notes on particular points of interest to consider in analysis. Interviews were unstructured and open ended but the scene had been set by the introductory letter and questionnaire. As noted above, interviewees were initially encouraged to comment on the questionnaire, to amplify and clarify responses and to give specific examples and illustrations of points made.

The methodological status of the interview account has been extensively discussed in the literature on sociological method. May (1997) summarised some of these arguments, observing that 'Interviews are used as a resource for understanding how individuals make sense of their social world and act within it.' (1997:129) but stressing the need to analyse interview data with a sensitivity to motivations, reasons and social identities. Interview accounts may be inaccurate (accidentally or deliberately). They may be incomplete: while genuinely reflecting the experience of the interviewee, there may be aspects of the phenomena under discussion of which the interviewee was not aware.

Harré and Secord (1972) proposed that: 'The things that people say about themselves should be taken seriously as reports of data relevant to phenomena that *really exist* and which are *relevant* to the explanation of behaviour...It is through reports of feelings, plans, intentions, beliefs, reasons and so on that the meanings of social behaviour and the rules underlying social acts can be discovered.'(1972:7) - but also noted: .'..the feeling, mood or emotion, opinion, belief or intention avowed may not exist; or the feeling ascribed may not really be felt; or the opinion reported may not really be held...How can we tell which reports are of genuine states of mind which really did exist, and which reports pseudo-memories generated by the demand for commentary in a justificatory context?'(1972:107)

They suggested that '..there are many cases in which a certain sort of remark is not just a sign of, or a report of state of mind, but is a manifestation of that state of mind itself.' (1972:107), using the example of expressions of complaint being intimately associated with a state of discontent since such a state is manifested by complaint: the verbal complaint may therefore be taken as an indication of the complainer's actual state. This recognition of the situated nature of interview accounts and their vocabulary is similar to the arguments of Mills (1940) who proposed that the quest for a 'reality' underlying expressed motives for action was fruitless: 'There is no way to plumb behind verbalization into an individual..' (1940:910). Mills suggested that the examination of the 'vocabularies of motive' associated with particular situated actions was of sociological interest as these 'stabilize and guide behaviour and expectation of the reactions of others' (1940:911).[16]

Czarniawska-Joerges (1992) noted that 'the interview can be seen as the most accessible technique for research in organizations' (1992:199) and observed that language is a particular difficulty as the interviewer does not share the common understandings which underlie the use of language in specific settings and may not recognise this: she suggested that 'continuous comparative analysis' is a technique that can be used to reveal gaps in understanding and decode meanings. She reiterated the question posed by Harré and Secord: '..even if we know that what we reach are only representations, how do we know that these are the representations that guide the action and not just the representations produced for our benefit during the interview?' (1992:201)

Her answer is that we do not and cannot. She also noted: '..analysts do not have to choose one version of reality as correct or introduce their own version as the right one: instead, one learns to deal with diversity by trying to understand its roots.'(1992:206)

Holstein and Gubrium (1997) observed that texts offering advice on interviewing perpetuate the picture of the interviewee as a 'vessel-of-answers' and urged a style of active interviewing that recognises that: '..the validity of answers derives not from their correspondence to meanings held within the respondent, but from their ability to convey situated experiential realities in terms that are locally comprehensible.'(1997:117)

These discussions argue for an analytic and interpretive approach to the use of interview data, recognising their situated nature and taking into account contextual and motivational factors: this is the approach adopted in this study, which demonstrates the range of differing understandings of audit committee activity, in order to explore the gap between the 'public' rhetoric and individual experience.

3.6   HOW ARE STORIES TO BE UNDERSTOOD? THE PROCESS OF ANALYSIS AND INTERPRETATION

The research method used has been informed by the grounded theory approach as developed by Glaser and Strauss (1967) and Strauss and Corbin (1990) and explicated in the context of accounting research by Parker and Roffey (1997). Analysis and preliminary interpretation of the data proceeded simultaneously with data collection.[17] Transcription of tapes, while time consuming, allowed the opportunity to search for important categories on an ongoing basis through immersion in the interview data. Transcripts were read and reread in conjunction with observational notes and minutes. Frequent rereading of transcripts, notes and listening to tapes generated more notes of an analytic nature, leading to the development of categories. The importance of categories was identified by consideration of the following inter-connected factors:

- frequency of mention by interviewees: both high and low frequency were considered as indicators
- context: expectations of both interviewer and interviewee about the context of the discussion, inevitably framed by the questionnaire and/or the source of the original contact
- approach – for example, did the interviewee introduce the topic, wish to exclude it or return to it?

As further interviews were undertaken, particular categories and areas of interest developing from the analysis could be pursued more specifically. In some cases developing ideas were discussed with subsequent interviewees (although this was problematic because of confidentiality). Preliminary ideas were discussed with colleagues and presented in conference papers (Spira, 1997a, 1997b)

The initial research question derived from the audit committee literature was broadly framed: what makes an audit committee effective? However, as demonstrated in chapter 2, a critical reading of the literature indicated the problematic nature of arriving at a definition of effectiveness and interviewees highlighted this both in their questionnaire responses and in subsequent discussion (see section 3.5 above). This led to a closer focus in the interviews on what effectiveness meant to the individuals concerned in an attempt to explore Collier's question: why have audit committees been established so widely when their effectiveness remains unproven? (Collier, 1996)

While supporting the intention of the Cadbury Code, interviewees shared a degree of scepticism about the capacity of the audit committee to achieve the Cadbury objectives. This was expressed strongly with regard to fraud and frequent reference was made to Robert Maxwell: 'Maxwell would be Maxwell whatever'(Chris Tracker, Scrimshaw plc); 'I don't believe that internal control reporting will ever catch a Maxwell' (Robin Dunston, Scrimshaw plc); 'You know all this will not catch the crooks like Maxwell' (Alex Anderson, Glengarry plc); 'I should think that with Maxwell an audit committee was desirable – it may even have existed but ... it must have been ineffectual because of the dominance of one man' (Henry Morton, Runic plc). However, there was some support for the potential of the audit committee to inhibit and deter.[18] A gap was thus perceived between the public assertions of the value of audit committees as expressed in Cadbury and the private beliefs of the individuals involved in their activities. This gives a different spin to Collier's question: how do participants make audit committees 'work' if they do not believe that they can be effective? The reframing of the question from a causal 'why?' to 'how?' emphasises the use of an interpretive approach in the study.

As the ongoing analysis revealed increasingly complex and dynamic interrelationships among audit committee participants, a theoretical perspective which would suitably frame these networks was sought. The next chapter explains the analytic approach of actor-network theory and its appropriateness for this task.

Chapter 4
NOTES ON THE THEORY OF ACTOR-NETWORKS

This chapter outlines the main concepts and analytical tools employed in actor-network theory through a discussion of studies which have developed and used the idea of 'moments of translation.' The relevance of this concept to the analysis of audit committee activity is demonstrated. The selected studies discussed in this section explain, illustrate and apply ANT concepts and demonstrate the variety of areas in which tools of ANT may be appropriately used. This study makes particular use of the concept and vocabulary of translation to analyse the engagement of audit committee participants in corporate governance issues.

4.1   WHAT IS ACTOR-NETWORK THEORY?

The ideas underlying actor-network theory (ANT) - also described as the sociology of translation - were initially developed and applied by a group of sociologists studying the sociology of science at the Centre de Sociologie de l'Innovation at the Ecole Nationale Superieure des Mines de Paris. Concepts of ANT have been developed in a series of papers[19], including Callon's account of the scallop beds in St Brieuc Bay (Callon, 1986), discussed in detail below: they have also been applied in a variety of studies, including an examination of the role of the GP in the UK cervical screening programme (Singleton and Michael, 1993), an analysis of the historical development of schools of thought in economics (Yonay, 1994), an account of the introduction of new accounting systems in three Australian hospitals (Chua, 1995) and an account of an attempt to introduce a new budgeting system in a university (Ezzamel 1994).

In using these concepts to illuminate the role and activities of the audit committee, an outline of ANT tools is offered, rather than a full critical analysis of the theory. However, it should be noted that the theory is not without its critics (Collins and Yearley,1992). A sympathetic account of the philosophical approach underlying ANT is offered by Lee and Brown (1994).

This study does not purport to be a complete ANT analysis since this would be particularly difficult to write up under the condition of confidentiality under which data was collected. Neither does the use of ANT concepts in this study imply a full acceptance of all substantive tenets proposed by actor-network theorists: this point is elaborated in section 4.2 below. However, the analytical framework offered by the actor-network perspective allows an interpretation of audit committee activities which highlights the dynamics of the relationships among participants and their influence on audit committee behaviour.

This chapter outlines the concepts of ANT through a discussion of several studies which have introduced and employed these concepts. The appropriateness of these concepts to the analysis of audit committee operations is indicated.

4. 2   PUNCTUALISATION: NETWORKS OF NETWORKS

Law (1992) outlined the key points of actor-network theory, describing it as a form of sociological analysis concerned with 'the mechanics of power'. The theory uses the 'metaphor of the heterogeneous network' to suggest that 'society, organisations, agents and machines are all *effects* generated in patterned networks of diverse (not simply human) materials.' (1992: 380) This reflects the development of the theory within the sociology of science, in that it emphasises that the 'networks of the social' that generate these effects include non-human actors.

Law observed that our interactions with other people are mediated through objects which influence these interactions and relationships e.g. text, computers: the argument of actor-network theory is that the 'social order' depends as much on the influence of these materials as on human influence.

Thus, if the materials disappeared, so would social order, so objects and people may be equally important in the maintenance of social order. Law emphasised that this does not imply 'an ethical stance': to treat people and machines as equally important in this analysis is not the same as suggesting that people should be treated as machines. What it does imply is that people 'are who they are because they are a patterned network of heterogeneous materials.'(1992:381) The theory argues that although the inner skills of individuals are important, 'social agents are never located in bodies and bodies alone'. Thus: ' thinking, acting, writing, loving, earning - all the attributes that we normally ascribe to human beings, are generated in networks that pass through and ramify both within and beyond the body.' (1992:384)

However, this view of non-human actors has not necessarily been fully endorsed by others employing an ANT approach. Chua (1995) observes that to: '..present inanimate objects such as computer software or hardware as actors which are identical to human agents...reifies machines and technologies in a way which detracts from the purposive activities of their designers. It is people who make up accounting numbers in specific ways to try and achieve certain objectives. Software, by contrast, has neither interest nor agency.' (1995:117)

The analysis in this study follows Chua in that it does not grant full actor status to objects. This is not to underestimate the power of, for example, a document such as a Financial Reporting Standard (FRS) in strengthening a network, but in this study such power is viewed as resulting from the use of the document by human actors.

Law then discussed why these networks are not always visible or of overt concern in social interaction and suggested that, in order to avoid dealing with the complexity that the network view opens up before us, '*network patterns that are widely performed are often those that can be punctualised*'. (Law's italics -1992:385) Punctualisation is a simplifying assumption: if a network acts as a single block, it is replaced by the action itself and the 'seemingly simple author of that action'.[20] The resources of the network may then be used without dealing with the underlying complexities. However, Law emphasised that 'punctualisation is always precarious': it is a process or effect, not a permanent state: 'Another way of saying this is to note that the bits and pieces assembled pro tem into an order are constantly liable to break down, or make off on their own. Thus, analysis of ordering struggle is central to actor-network theory.'(1992:386)

The process which generates the ordering effects - 'devices, agents, institutions or organizations' - is known as *translation*, implying that one thing – e.g. an actor - may stand for another – e.g. a network. The process of translation renders the network into a single punctualized actor and is concealed, along with the network, behind the actor.

How is translation effected? The actors comprising networks all offer innate resistance to ordering - how is this resistance overcome in the process of translation? Law noted that the exercise of power in this regard contains 'more than hint of Machiavelli'.[21] The process of translation is best understood through an illustrative example.

4. 3   HOW NETWORKS FORM AND RE-FORM: THE CONCEPT AND PROCESS OF 'TRANSLATION'

Callon (1986) provided a detailed illustration of the process of translation, in an account which illustrated that: '..the capacity of certain actors to get other actors - whether they be human beings, institutions or natural entities - to comply with them depends on a complex web of interrelations in which Society and Nature are intertwined.'(1986:201)

His story centred on the decline of the scallop population of St Brieuc Bay, the consequent threat to the livelihoods of the local fishermen, and the proposal of a group of researchers of a method to deal with this problem. Callon identified four stages or 'moments of translation' during the process by which these researchers developed their influence over this situation.

The researchers had visited Japan where a mechanism for intense cultivation of scallops had been developed, using towlines with netted bags which protect scallop larvae and allow them to establish themselves. They wished to investigate the possibility of using this method in StBrieuc but the French scallops were of a different species to those bred in Japan and the lack of detailed knowledge about the development of scallops in general meant that answers to questions about the viability of a project to restock St Brieuc Bay could not be presented with any authority. The central question was: would the French scallops anchor themselves to the netted bags in the same way as the Japanese species?

Callon argued that the initial formulation of the problem by the researchers gave them power over those they defined as actors in this situation (the fishermen, scientific colleagues and the scallops). The statement of the problem through a single question 'is enough to involve a whole series of actors by establishing their identities and the links between them.' (1986:205) The researchers then consolidated that power by defining themselves as an 'obligatory passage point', siting themselves at a controlling point within network processes. They demonstrated that the interests of the actors lay in the proposed research programme and that the actors needed to work together to achieve this. Callon defined this overall process as '*problematisation*' - the first 'moment of translation'.

The next significant stage involves locking the actors into place through a process of '*interessement*'. The actors may choose or refuse to participate in the programme: how can the researchers ensure their co-operation? It is important to recognise that each actor is also part of other networks, other problematisations, which will influence their desire to participate. Interessement implies the interposition of an actor between such other links in order to gain influence: thus A interests B by destroying or weakening links between B and C, D etc., and also by redefining B in the context of the relationship between A and B - a further dissociation from C, D etc. 'For all the groups involved, the interessement helps corner the entities to be enrolled. In addition, it attempts to interrupt all potential competing associations and to construct a system of alliances.' (1986:211)

In Callon's example, the devices of interessement are the towlines (for the scallops), texts (scientific papers) and conversations with the scientific colleagues and the fishermen.

The third stage is described as '*enrolment*' - 'the group of multilateral negotiations, trials of strength and tricks that accompany the interessements and enable them to succeed.'(1986:211) Enrolment of the scallops involved dealing with currents, predatory parasites and other technical issues. Enrolment of scientific colleagues was based on evidence from the research and the enrolment of the scallops. The fishermen were not directly involved in any negotiations, being prepared to wait for the outcome of the scientific process: their enrolment was not resisted. As Callon observed: 'This example illustrates the different possible ways in which actors are enrolled: physical violence (against the predators), seduction, transaction, and consent without discussion.' (1986:214)

The fourth stage is described as '*mobilisation*' and focuses on issues of representation. If some scallop larvae anchor, will all do so? If some scientific colleagues are convinced of the worth of the research programme, will all be? If some fishermen support the project of restocking the bay, will all do so? Callon argued that in each case the general community is 'constructed by interposed spokesmen' and that *chains of intermediaries* - the counting of larvae and conversion into graphs in reports, the election of fishermen delegates, the discussion at conferences of scientific papers - result in these spokesmen. The process enables previously dispersed groups - scallops, fishermen and scientists - to mobilise and come together to resolve a problem. However, Callon emphasised that this structure cannot be viewed as permanent in any way: '..this consensus and the alliances which it implies can be contested at any moment.' (1986:218) To demonstrate this, he traced the disintegration of the network: in subsequent years the scallop larvae did not attach and grow - they were swept away by 'a crowd of other actors' - the predators, currents and water temperatures from which the researchers initially managed to detach them through the process of interessement. Scientific colleagues became sceptical. A group of impatient fishermen chose to fish a newly established group of scallops, betraying their representatives who had agreed to restraint so that the long term programme would assure future supplies.

Callon emphasised the link between translation and displacement: the story of St Brieuc Bay illustrates displacement at every stage of translation. During problematisation, the fishermen were influenced to move from a preoccupation with short term interests to share the view of the researchers about a long term project. During interessement and enrolment, the larvae were captured within the nets, against the force of the currents. During mobilisation, the groups which were represented by the smaller groups were all displaced and brought to a scientific conference where the researchers claim to be their spokesmen. Subsequent unpredictable displacements led to the actors changing and bypassing the researchers - the *obligatory passage point* of the research project - thus leading to the network's disintegration.

Translation is also 'to express in one's own language what others say and want' (1986:223) - to establish oneself as a spokesman - thus 'the researchers translated the fishermen, the scallops and the scientific community'(1986:223). Callon concluded: 'Translation is the mechanism by which the social and natural worlds progressively take form. The result is a situation in which certain entities control others. Understanding what sociologists generally call power relationships means describing the way in which actors are defined, associated and simultaneously obliged to remain faithful to their alliances. The repertoire of translation is not only designed to give a symmetrical and tolerant description of a complex process which constantly mixes together a variety of social and natural entities. It also permits an explanation of how a few obtain the right to express and to represent the many silent actors of the social and natural worlds they have mobilized.' (1986:224)

4. 4   OTHER ANT CONCEPTS: MICRO AND MACRO PERSPECTIVES, BLACK BOXES AND WARS

One important argument of ANT theorists is that ANT allows the same tools to be used for analysis at micro and macro level (Callon and Latour, 1981), thus collapsing what they view as an artificial distinction based on size which obscures and oversimplifies the nature of power and influence proposed by the theory. Networks are formed and strengthened through links forged by processes of problematisation, interessement and enrolment but a chain is only as strong as its weakest link and the fragility of these networks is always acknowledged. The size of a network is immaterial - its strength is founded elsewhere.

Callon and Law (1989) returned to the story of the scallops of St Brieuc Bay and examined how the researchers enrolled their sponsoring government organisation, French consumers of scallops, the scientific community and local government organisation to create the context and the *negotiation space* for the subsequent creation of the network in which the fishermen and scallops were enrolled. This macro-level enrolment involved manipulating networks which already existed: scallop consumers, for example, had already been effectively simplified by the production of statistics relating to their consumption of this delicacy and the researchers re-defined this network, focusing solely on their demand for the product for the purposes of the study. Callon and Law described this process as *preforming* a network: 'such allies [existing networks] are mobilized without undue effort, but the fact that they are mobilized in turn leads them to change.'(1989:61) This process takes place within a 'centre of translation' where resources are drawn from existing networks to create a new one, usually on the basis of some type of reciprocal return between networks. Law and Callon (1992) illustrated this in their analysis of the TSR2 development, a large British aerospace project. This defined the existence of a global network which provided resources to generate a negotiation space for the development of a local network to generate intermediaries - particularly an aircraft - which would be returned to the global network. Law and Callon argued that the project failed because actors in both networks were able to avoid the obligatory passage point between the two networks and thus subvert control by the managers of the project.

Callon and Latour (1981) explained how micro actors become macro actors, using the concept of *the black box*: 'An actor grows with the number of relations he or she can put, as we say, in black boxes. A black box contains that which no longer needs to be reconsidered. The more elements one can place in black boxes - modes of thought, habits, forces and objects - the broader the construction one can raise. Of course, black boxes never remain fully closed or properly fastened....but macro-actors can do *as if* they were closed and dark.' (1981:285)

Yonay (1994) used this concept in his analysis of competing schools of economic thought. Accepted ideas become black boxes and contribute to the development of scientific paradigms or schools of thought which Yonay viewed as actor-networks. He observed that: 'The process of making a black box does not require consensus of opinion....new knowledge does not have to be accepted by all (or by a large majority) in order to be considered as a black box. It is a sufficient condition that it is a constituent in *any* ongoing network.' (1994:42)

Thus acceptance within a small group may be enough to give such ideas power which can then be grasped by actors through enrolment in their networks.

Singleton and Michael (1993) used a complex metaphor of film cameras mounted on scaffolding to contrast their own approach to ANT, which focuses on the flux and instability of networks, with that of Callon and Latour which, they imply, offers a more starkly determined approach to networks: '..problems arise when the singularity of the entities within the analytic narrative threatens to occlude the indeterminacy and the ambivalence of those entities and of the associations into which they are tied. Perhaps this is linked to the recurrent metaphor of war that runs through actor-network theory: certainly, it often seems as if these accounts are structured by magnificent victories and disastrous defeats...An alternative metaphor might be that of permanent reform; the world we wish to examine is one of inherent instability and incessant skirmishes.' (1993:232)

Ezzamel (1994) used Foucault's model of power and the concept of translation to examine an attempt by central management within a university to effect changes in resource allocation which was successfully opposed by other groups. He described translation as: '.. the process through which an agency enrols other agencies in order to forge alliances in situations of organisational struggle and conflict. The process of 'translation' specifically refers to how agents transform phenomena into resources and resources into networks of power which seek to form alliances and coalitions, to engineer antagonism and to constitute interests.' (1994:218) - and used Callon's articulation of the translation process to analyse the dynamics of power within the institution.

Callon's version of translation process will be used in the subsequent analysis and may be summarised thus:

1. PROBLEMATISATION: an actor seeking to develop influence in order to solve a problem establishes the nature of the problem and its own position. A 'centre of translation' takes form within a space between existing networks.

2. INTERESSEMENT: the actor interposes itself between the actors it seeks to enrol and the rival associations of these actors in other networks; the process also involves redefining these actors in terms of the newly developing network. Interessement devices may be expressed in verbs such as 'corner', 'lure', 'trap'.

3. ENROLMENT: the outcome of successful interessement, described by Callon (1987:211) as '..the group of multilateral negotiations, trials of strength and tricks that accompany the interessements and enable them to succeed'. 'Chains of intermediaries' are created through the use of a variety of methods which may include physical violence, seduction, and transaction. The process may also involve the 'stacking' of 'black boxes', representing accepted facts. An 'obligatory passage point' may be established which allows control of actors/intermediaries moving between networks.

4. MOBILISATION (also simplification, punctualisation): the original actor can now represent its new network in the area of desired influence to solve the problem. Callon (1987:94) noted that: 'Behind each associated entity there hides another set of entities that it more or less effectively draws together'.

5. DISINTEGRATION: competing interessement devices enrol actors in other networks where they are redefined.

Thus, through the process of translation, A defines B's identity for the purpose of A's network: this redefinition of identity is the core process in the creation of networks. Michael (1996:54) expressed the process in terms of the following statements: 'This is what you want to be' (interessement) 'We are the ones who can help you become that' (translation) 'Grant your obedience by your own consent' (enrolment)

Michael observed that this process takes place within the 'geography' of 'obligatory points of passage' which represent 'unavoidable conduits' and 'narrative bottlenecks' through which entities must pass 'in order to articulate both their identity and their *raison d'etre.*' (1996:54)

4. 5   AUDIT COMMITTEES FROM AN ANT PERSPECTIVE

Chua (1995) argued that ANT concepts are useful in accounting research because they enable us to study:
'..how a certain notion of reality came to be socially constructed and how and why a fact-building network emerged and survived Machiavellian-like - what are the human and non-human resources, stratagems, ploys and persuasive strategies used by actors with divergent interests to initiate, maintain or, in certain cases, destroy knowledge networks? Who are the allies who/which are mobilized, how are competitors cut down and conquered, which authorities are used to stack particular arguments, how are stronger software or formulae built to cover as many contexts as possible? In what ways are appeals to truth and truthfulness mobilized by fact-builders and to what effect? Such questions are useful because they focus analysis on the *processes* of fact-fabrication and socio-political ties that hold together to form truth.'(1995:115)

ANT studies, originally developed in the area of scientific development and practice, often require lengthy description and explication of complex technical detail. It is a method of analysis particularly suited to the examination of large technical projects where development over a lengthy time period may be traced and where considerable documentation exists and is accessible. This approach would be suitable for undertaking an analysis of the development of audit committees over a lengthy time frame and in an international context, which would extend and develop the ideas introduced in this more limited study. The networks examined in this study link into this wider network: the perspective would change if one selected as a network node 'The Cadbury Report' rather than 'the finance director of X plc' but the links may still be traced using the same tools of analysis. Thus ANT may be used to analyse networks at both macro and micro levels and to trace the interconnections between the two.

This study focuses on the negotiation space created by actors in individual companies (by drawing on the wider networks of the UK corporate governance framework) and examines the ways in which, within this space, networks form and re-form around and within the audit committee as it undertakes its allotted tasks. Before proceeding to consider the data generated within the study, it is appropriate to consider the broader corporate governance context, within which audit committees operate, from an ANT perspective.

The Cadbury Committee was established in 1991 by the Financial Reporting Council, the London Stock Exchange and the accountancy profession: the rationale for this is contained in the Introduction to the Committee's Report (Cadbury Committee,1992: 2.1) 'Its sponsors were concerned at the perceived low level of confidence both in financial reporting and in the ability of the auditors to provide the safeguards which users of company reports sought and expected.'

Recent financial scandals such as Polly Peck[22] had exposed the accountancy profession to unfavourable press comment and the need for public action was important. The situation very closely paralleled that surrounding the establishment of the UK accounting standard setting machinery in 1970: Robson (1991) analysed this using the concept of translation. He observed that: '..the 'problems' and 'worries' concerning accounting and auditing practices were taken up and set against a particular professional discourse that defined the accounting profession in the U.K. as a self-regulatory body. In the presence of prompting by state agencies, a professional elite translated the 'problems' articulated by others into their own terms and ideals.' (1991:566)

Robson also noted that the establishment of the Accounting Standards Steering Committee (ASSC) in 1970 followed a lead given in the United States where the Accounting Principles Board had already been set up:
'The bounded discursive interpretation by the profession of the problematization of accounting practices drew upon an existing policy legacy. The translation of accounting problems to the discourse of

accounting principles and standards allowed the profession to invoke a response for which a major international and professional precedent existed: the formation of the Accounting Principles Board. As such the 'solution' put forward by the profession displayed an institutional isomorphism (Meyer and Rowan, 1977) by assuming common problems, and following the practices of other bodies and professions.' (1991:565)

In the same way, the Treadway Commission in the United States (Treadway Commission, 1987) provided a pattern for Cadbury to follow.

The parallel extends further: the ASSC was replaced by the Accounting Standards Committee and reviews of the standard setting process were undertaken by committees headed by Watts, McKinnon and Dearing during the twenty years up to the establishment of the Accounting Standards Board in 1990 (Davies et al, 1999, 26-34). Similarly, the Cadbury Committee was followed by the Greenbury Committee (Greenbury, 1995) and the Hampel Committee (Hampel, 1998). Although as Yonay (1994) has pointed out (see section 4.4 above) it is not necessary for a particular position to be widely accepted for it to be 'black boxed', it would appear that there is a need for regular 'maintenance' of interessement devices such as the accounting standard setting machinery and the Cadbury Code, addressing criticism and enabling the devices to remain useful in the wider professional arena, as well as at the individual company level which is examined in this study.

Thus the setting up of the Cadbury Committee was a problematisation by its sponsors of the financial aspects of corporate governance. The Cadbury Code offered a solution at the level identified by Power (1997) as programmatic, in contrast to the more practical technical level. In discussing the development of formal guidance in the area of financial auditing, Power observed that, at the programmatic level: 'Much of what goes on here is not guidance for practitioners at all but a certain kind of institutionalized presentation of the knowledge base of financial auditing. It must be 'practical' enough to look like guidance to outsiders but not so practical that these outsiders could replicate or judge it without the help of insiders. In this way disturbances to the system, in the form of new demands, or old demands with a new rhetoric, can be managed by transforming the unfamiliar and intractable into the familiar and possible.' (1997:25)

Thus the mystique of financial auditing is preserved and the accountancy profession maintains its power in the same manner identified by Robson above. The effect of the Cadbury Code may be similarly perceived.

As Power commented: 'Not only is the essential obscurity of financial auditing undisturbed but there is a presumed relation between disclosure and corporate activity which is highly problematic.' (1997:55)

He quoted Keasey and Wright (1993:301): 'Audit committees might be a means not of more effective reporting but of avoiding scrutiny.' – a similar conclusion to Collier(1996). Collier's explanation of his 'curious phenomenon' can be interpreted through the ANT lens: large public companies[23] are prepared to carry the costs of audit committee establishment and to enrol, throwing in their lot with Cadbury's sponsors (principally the accounting profession), to avoid the possible burden of legislation and detailed scrutiny. As later chapters will demonstrate, at company level the requirements of the Code with regard to audit committees can be used as an interessement/enrolment device by groups and individuals with particular objectives.

The Cadbury support for audit committees is based on the assumption that the quality of financial reporting is closely related to the independence of external auditors[24]. The assumption underpinning Cadbury[25] is that this 'quality' is potentially threatened by attempts by the executive directors to enrol the auditors in employing accounting policies which, while strictly legitimate within current generally accepted accounting practice, fall into 'grey' areas and might be viewed pejoratively as 'creative accounting or 'aggressive earnings management'. These might be policies based on a specific reading of the existing regulation which follows the 'letter' rather than the 'spirit' intended, as in the use of off balance sheet finance, (discussed by Griffiths, 1995) or policies which push against the boundaries of acceptable practice where none has yet been determined[26], as in the case of accounting for brands (Griffiths, 1995). At Glengarry plc the finance director described such policies as 'sporty treatments'. Enrolment devices include the threat of losing the company as an audit client (and possibly as a provider of other services) or an adjustment to audit fees.

The Cadbury solution is to interpose the audit committee, composed of NEDs, between the auditors and the executive directors. NEDs – objective, independent, theoretically with a perspective more closely aligned with shareholders interests - form the channel of communication between the auditors and the executives, in theory providing an *obligatory passage point* through which the auditors are enrolled into their 'independent' network, preventing direct influence by executive management. We thus see the board composed of two distinct networks, each concerned to enrol the auditors.'

However, in situations where obligatory passage points can be circumvented, networks disintegrate (Law and Callon,1992). In order to do their work, external auditors must deal on a regular basis with the finance director. Good working relationships may be as powerful an enrolment device as the threats outlined above[27], as will be demonstrated in chapter 7. Further, the main source of information for the audit committee is often the finance director: he or she thus controls the obligatory passage point between the two networks of the board. Where the audit committee chair has a finance background, it is very likely that the audit committee chair and the finance director will form a good working relationship. Thus the auditors may equally well be enrolled by management, despite apparent compliance with Cadbury.

This sense of competition or contest for enrolment of actors permeates the literature on audit committees. Corrin (1993:81) used a dramatic analogy: 'The whole report is like a script for a 'soap' where the non-executive director is cast as saint, the auditor is a tarnished guardian angel, and the executive director is a villain.'

It also links to the metaphor of surprise or threat, particularly evident in the practitioner literature. The theme of actor-network studies as analyses of conflict outlined above (although criticised by Singleton and Michael) intuitively suggests that ANT is an appropriate analytical tool to examine this area. It also suggests that a suitable focus for consideration would be how audit committees achieve consensus on contentious issues, an area examined in detail in chapter 7.

Identification of problematisation, interessement and enrolment processes illuminates the pattern of relationships between participants and the shifting balance of power and influence surrounding audit committee operation. Participants' stories focused on the event of the audit committee meeting. The next chapter examines the role of the audit committee meeting through an ANT lens, exploring its use as an interessement and enrolment device.

Chapter 5
THE AUDIT COMMITTEE MEETING: A PRIVATE PERFORMANCE FOR A PUBLIC AUDIENCE

In chapter 3 a contradiction was identified between participants' scepticism about the ability of audit committees to function in the way that Cadbury envisaged, and their support for the practical value of audit committees. In this chapter this contradiction is explored through an examination of the functions of the audit committee meeting, using the approach of actor-network theory outlined in chapter 4. The analysis demonstrates that the ceremonial performance of the committee's existence is used as an interessement and enrolment device by the full board to legitimate the company in the eyes of external suppliers of finance, as well as a symbolic deterrent to fraud and incompetence within the company.

5.1   THE AUDIT COMMITTEE MEETING AS A CEREMONIAL PERFORMANCE

In seeking to understand the ways in which the audit committee meeting acts as a resource in building and maintaining the external and internal networks of the company, the enabling aspects of the ceremonial[28] of meeting process become apparent as will be demonstrated.

However, participants interviewed were conscious of criticism such as that expressed by Corrin (1993) and did not wish the meetings to be described as 'ceremonial' or 'ritual', sensitive to implications of superficiality. Finance directors emphasised this - Chris Tracker at Scrimshaw described the process of preparing for the audit committee meeting as: '.. making sure that the audit committee just doesn't become a non-event, that it actually has teeth, that actually the company benefits from it as well as the individuals. I think a few years ago audit committees were a bit like that when they first started..'

Alex Anderson at Glengarry commented: '..meetings which are strictly scripted are actually pretty unproductive, we can all read out the papers and everyone nods and says yes, agreed, is not actually that productive because where you've got real issues, where you clearly present the facts, you know, if someone has a question they're prepared to ask it or a different point of view that is stated.... I've certainly had clients where I was quite concerned about the way audit committees worked, where there's quite a lot of friction particularly with the finance director, you know, with a finance director who's actually trying not to be open with the audit committee, trying to keep things - pushing it under the carpet rather than actually explain that there was an issue here and we did need to address what was to be done about it..'

Both Chris and Alex emphasised that their audit committees engaged in substantive activity rather than empty ceremonial. Max Tinker, however, offered a frank description of his experience as a recently appointed non-executive director chairing the audit committee at North Eastern plc, which implied that the established pattern there was a ceremonial performance: 'The thing that I've noticed is I go along to North Eastern and there's plenty of board papers but the background - you know you've got no background, the executive directors make a recommendation and you're pretty well expected to say 'yes'..

Although Max indicated that this was not, in his view, a satisfactory state of affairs, Roy Milford described his experience as an external auditor where NEDs had apparently colluded willingly in similar situations: '..yes, there are audit committees who don't want to know a thing, they just want to show up..'

It is interesting to observe that these interviewees acknowledged experience of faults and failures in audit committee processes which made such committees examples of automatic 'rubber-stamping', but their illustrations were always related to experiences in companies other than their current principal affiliation. These stories were also related alongside stories of their current audit committee roles, which revealed participants' manipulation of aspects of audit committee meetings (examined in chapter 6) that could be interpreted as having equivalent outcomes to those condemned above, effectively neutralising the audit committee in the terms envisaged by Cadbury.

From an ANT perspective it is possible to discern the role of ceremonial as a powerful interessement and enrolment device in itself, as well as a process which enables other such devices to be brought into play. Kunda (1992:257) summarised three approaches to ritual: the integrative view of ritual as behaviour which serves to reinforce group solidarity, the conflict perspective of writers such as Lukes (1975) who argue that ritual is used to achieve and maintain power by dominant groups and an interpretive approach which sees ritual as 'a dramatic form that may contain both conflictual and integrative processes.' It is the third approach which informs this discussion.[29]

If the audit committee meeting is viewed as a ceremonial performance, who are the performers? Many people may attend an audit committee meeting: apart from the committee members, the finance director and the external auditors will normally be present, as will others, such as internal auditors, whose activities are of close interest to the committee. All board members are usually entitled to attend if they wish. The audit committee members will probably be outnumbered by the additional participants and this must inevitably influence their behaviour. The principal form of performance that is revealed in participants' stories is the asking of questions: this is discussed in more detail in chapter 8.

Descriptions of individual 'performances' at meetings were notable because they were so infrequent: Simon Middleton, the internal auditor at Glengarry, described the tense relationship between Martin Johnson and the company chairman and noted that 'the other NEDs - all important people in their own companies - have to sit and watch what goes on between the two of them.' He described the audit committee chair as 'worrying at issues like a dog with a bone' which frustrated the company chairman. At Runic, Henry Morton described an American NED who often dominated proceedings: '...you sit round the [Runic] board ... you hear [him]at great length.' Chris Tracker offered an unusual description of a meeting at Scrimshaw: 'It got very emotional at the last one when we were talking about technical requirements.'

However, in keeping with the general emphasis in their accounts on consensus and agreement[30], interviewees did not often relate stories about individual behaviour, even their own. When asked the question 'What happens at audit committee meetings?', most participants initially responded by describing agendas and the type of information provided for discussion.

They then continued to describe the other features of the meetings identified as 'ceremonial components' in section 5.5 below.

Three types of audience may be identified for the performance of audit committee ceremonial: those external to the company, those within the company but external to the committee meeting, and those who participate within the meeting itself. The integrative view of ritual would suggest that its primary importance is for those who participate: indeed, Schwartzman's anthropological study of meetings supports this approach (Schwartzman, 1989). She analysed meeting components in some detail and surveyed the literature on meetings in a variety of disciplines, commenting on the tendency of other studies to use the meeting as a tool to examine other issues such as decision-making, and highlighting the paucity of research which focuses on the meeting itself as a topic. However, although noting: 'After the fact, a meeting is objectified as it becomes a text for interpretation and may be 'read' as tangible evidence of organisational activity *or* inactivity.'(1989:83), she did not consider in detail the role of the meeting as a symbol for those not directly involved.

A similar emphasis is found in the work of Mangham (1986:127) who used the metaphor of theatrical performance to explore interactions at board meetings, characterising them as improvisations around commonly understood scripts: '...realizing in the performance a form of ritual. Not an empty form, as so many of the usages of the term now imply; rather a celebration and a grounding of the relations which obtain between those concerned.' He suggested that such performances help to define individuals' concepts of themselves: 'Interpersonal behaviour...is enacted to maintain or enhance each actor's relative comfort, security and freedom from anxiety.'

However, the potential for the influence of ceremonial beyond the group directly involved has been acknowledged in other studies. Kunda (1992:157) spoke of a 'secondary audience'. Brown (1994:863) observed that: 'Symbolic action and myth making are important means by which individuals and groups seek to legitimate their privileged power relations and actions and indeed to guarantee their organisation's continued successful existence. This depends on the support of internal and external constituencies, and accordingly, processes of organisational legitimation are directed to both sets of stakeholders.'

Baumann (1992:99) suggested that rituals may be addressed to 'Others' and may indeed 'serve to negotiate the differing relationships of its participants with these 'Others''. He further observed that it may be useful to view rituals as 'resources competed for and used by various constituencies'. This supports the view of audit committee meetings as interessement and enrolment devices used by both the board and the individual participants.

Two types of performance may then be identified: performance *of* the meeting and performance *in* the meeting. Performance *in* the meeting will be explored in chapter 6 by examining participants' use of the ceremonial aspects of the meeting in creating networks. The performance *of* the meeting and the audiences for that performance are discussed below.

5.2   THE ROLE OF THE AUDIT COMMITTEE MEETING: BEYOND THE COMPANY

From an ANT perspective, the performance of the audit committee meeting acts as an interessement and enrolment device both externally and internally.

Companies complying with the Cadbury Code give details of audit committee membership in their annual report, in accordance with appendix 4, paragraph 6(f). Such reports vary in the level of detail but all indicate that the audit committee has met during the year to transact appropriate business. Runic in 1995 reported : 'The audit committee meets regularly to review with the auditors the Group's annual report and interim results and also ensures that appropriate accounting policies and compliance procedures are in place.'

Scrimshaw's report for 1995 was similarly brief: 'The Audit Committee receives reports regularly from the Group Internal Audit Department and ensures that an objective and professional relationship is maintained between the Board and the external auditors.'

Glengarry in 1994 reported in considerable detail on the company's internal control system, including the following description of audit committee activity: 'The Audit Committee comprises four non-executive Directors. The Chairman and Finance Director normally attend the meetings but the Committee also meets with the external auditors without management present. The Committee operates under written terms of reference and its duties include the detailed review of financial statements prior to their recommendation to the Board for approval.'

In terms of Callon's 'moments of translation' (Callon, 1986) such reports, the public demonstration of the existence of the audit committee, may be viewed as *punctualisations* of the committee itself. The report then forms part of the package of accountability provided by the board of directors to the shareholders in the company annual report. This, in turn, acts as an interessement and enrolment device by demonstrating to those parties with an existing or potential relationship with the company that the company is concerned to establish high standards of corporate governance by complying with the Cadbury Code in this respect. This is likely to influence suppliers of finance, strengthening the network node of the company by increasing its available resources. Tsui et al (1994) and Felton et al (1996) both report evidence of this. Davis (1997) surveyed key corporate governance indicators in the UK, the US, France, Germany and Japan and observed: 'Corporate governance has become a significant factor considered by institutional investors when making world-wide investment decisions and tending ownership stakes...Many brokers and shareholders now compare ownership rights and governance characteristics as part of their routine due diligence reviews of companies. Some are under a mandate to do so. Others have come to the conviction that appropriate governance structures reduce risk and promote performance..'

Coombes and Watson (2000) identified the significant premiums investors would be willing to pay for well-governed companies ranging from 18% for UK/US companies to 28% in Latin America.

The public report of the existence and activity of the audit committee has a symbolic function in speaking to those who have or are contemplating a relationship with the company. It records the events of the time period covered by the report and offers the reassurance that the positive outcomes of such events will be repeated in the future: under the high standards of corporate governance symbolised by the audit committee's existence, resources contributed to the company will be efficiently and effectively managed with the promise of an appropriate return to the providers. Additionally, the activities of the audit committee offer a further reassurance, that the account of the company's activities may be relied upon – the auditors have, as a result of the protection of the audit committee, been able to report independently, free of any pressure from the management of the company. Ceremony and ritual emphasise stability and continuity. As Moore and Myerhoff (1977:24) observed: 'Since ritual is a good form for conveying a message as if it were unquestionable, it often is used to communicate those very things which are most in doubt...Action itself may be soothing ... Ceremony can make it appear that there is no conflict, only harmony, no disorder, only order, that if danger threatens, safe solutions are at hand..'

The ceremony of the annual financial reporting process is enhanced by the report of the audit committee's activities.

The audit committee meeting remains essentially private: many other meetings take place within a company but remain unreported externally. The reports describe regular audit committee meetings focussing on areas which carry risks for external parties: the reassurance lies not so much in the actual business conducted – external parties do not receive detailed minutes – but in the reports themselves. Only the fact of the meetings is a matter of public report: decisions and outcomes are not – the committee itself is not reporting[31] and there is no indication of precisely how the committee's objectives are achieved. The introduction of such reports is a recent addition to the package of disclosure relating to the accountability of directors and has been absorbed into the ceremonial format of such reports.

5.3 THE MEETING WITHIN THE MEETING: AN EVEN MORE PRIVATE ENCOUNTER

The private meeting between the external auditors and the audit committee referred to in Glengarry's report quoted above is considered to be good practice: 'The [audit] committee should have a discussion with the auditors, at least once a year, without executive board members present, to ensure there are no unresolved areas of concern.' (Cadbury Committee, 1992:70)

Such a meeting is intended as a public demonstration that the audit committee functions to support the independence of external auditor against any possible pressure from the executive management of the company. The meetings are not normally minuted, as Max Tinker, the finance director of Runic, described: '.. the fourth one [audit committee meeting in the year] might be a meeting just between the audit committee and the external auditors, but in fact they had a meeting after our last audit committee, and that's a private meeting, I don't know what's said there - things like, you know, 'Is Max Tinker doing a reasonable job? What do you really think about the accounts now that we've got them out of the way?' but I actually don't know and as far as I know there are no minutes of those meetings..'

Henry Morton indicated that Max did not need to be anxious about the content of such meetings: '..we always have a chat with the auditors at the end of audit committee meetings, when nobody else is there, about the audit committee, not that anything important particularly comes out of that, it's really striving to find out that there isn't anything that isn't being said really, and in the best ordered house that really doesn't happen, it certainly doesn't happen here ..'

Ronald Roberts noted that this was a recent introduction and speculated about the reasons for it:
'.. at the end of the audit committee meeting there [at Runic] they ask the executive directors to leave, so we and they can discuss whatever they want to discuss with us - now that has changed, it has only happened in the last year - they may want to say things very directly to us which they feel are possibly more embarrassing to say in front of the executive members and also they just want to make sure that we've got no burning issues that we couldn't say to the executives, which I would say would surprise me..... it may have changed because of the whole environment in which we're seen to be independent and so on...one of the non-executives is an American ....and I think it's the style probably in America more along, you know, having face to face chats, so we find it - I mean, it's quite useful, I think it's probably more useful for them [the audit committee] than it is for us. At Tiffin that doesn't happen, it doesn't happen directly, you know, we might have - the chairman of the audit committee may say: 'I want a one-to-one with you'- but it's not necessarily at the end of every meeting –' Can we just make sure that we have ten minutes, half an hour whatever with the auditors separately from the executives?'.. I think this is probably different because issues at [Runic] are complex ....and I think because of the complexities they just want to make sure that on a face to face that everyone makes sure that they are absolutely happy with what's going on.'

This account seems to indicate that the private meeting works as a comfort device for the audit committee - 'I think it's probably more useful for them than it is for us', '..they just want to make sure that on a face to face that everyone makes sure that they are absolutely happy with what's going on' - rather than the more conventional view that it supports the external auditor's independence. However, the comparison drawn between the two different companies should be considered in the light of the fact that, at the time of this interview, the same individual chaired the audit committees at Runic and at Tiffin, and the same accountancy firm audited both companies, the audit teams including the same audit partners. Good working relationships had been established and there was fairly regular informal contact between Henry Morton and the audit partners, as Henry Morton described: 'I meet XYZ socially anyway and also from time to time at other meetings and other occasions, when we meet we have chats and they would quite often ring me up about something or other and talk to me so, yes, communication's very good. Without it I think it would be very difficult to do it..'

In these particular circumstances, with very open channels of communication, the role of the private meeting appears to be entirely symbolic. At Glengarry, Alex Anderson described such meetings as 'routine': '..the other point to make is that the audit committee does from time to time see the auditors on their own without you know the executives present... I suppose typically it would happen at the end of the meeting and we'd all know about it, I mean it's a matter of routine..'

However, at Harrier, such a routine had not yet been established: '.. in most audit committees I've been involved with the finance director doesn't sort of stick around throughout the meeting - when I was an auditor I used to be alone with the audit committee, the finance function having left - here it's not quite like that - we tend not to go away ...' (Roy Milford)

This might perhaps be connected to Roy's specific situation as auditor-turned-finance director for this particular company. No audit committee existed at the time when he was the partner in charge of the company's audit. Harrier was, at the time of the interview, in the early stages of establishing procedures in accordance with Cadbury, having been until recently dominated by a single founding entrepreneur. It is possible that the institution of this private meeting is a part of the panoply of ceremonial 'good practice' which companies will adopt to reflect particular circumstances: certainly at Glengarry the public demonstration of high standards of corporate governance was of major concern, whereas at Harrier a certain amount of reluctance could be sensed in the context of complying with Cadbury. (Jeremy James, the deputy chairman was particularly outspoken in his contempt for audit committees, describing them as a 'complete waste of time, they know nothing about the company.')

Chris Tracker at Scrimshaw commented: 'Also we have a session we allow during the process for anybody to be thrown out who's not a member, so they will at certain times of the year choose to talk to the auditors on their own and so it's not just purely us saying 'Shut up, don't say that'..'

The use of the expression 'a session we allow' is of interest here: it implies that even this ultimate guarantee of external auditor independence is somehow within the gift of the executive directors.

Bob Cunningham, a very experienced audit committee chair and member of the Cadbury Committee, laid great emphasis on the importance of this private meeting, pointing out that he considered it so important that he would normally see the auditors privately before the audit committee meeting. He described the fact of the meeting, and its demonstration that the external auditors had a direct channel to the NEDs, as an important deterrent to fraud and incompetence, using the term 'prophylactic'.

The role of the private meeting between the audit committee and the external auditors illustrates both the symbolic nature of audit committee meetings and the use of this symbol in strengthening of a variety of networks that is taking place. The rhetoric presents this meeting as an important link to provide support for the external auditors and to prevent undue influence being exerted over them by the executive management of the company, but the external auditor at Runic saw this meeting as more useful to the audit committee, offering it comfort. The meeting is not minuted or mentioned in the company's annual report. It is a demonstration of good practice to and by both the external auditors and the members of the audit committee: the reassurance that those present are complying with the recommendations of the Cadbury Code -'doing the right thing' - acts as an enrolment device, strengthening the audit committee as a network.

Sections 2 and 3 have thus examined the way in which the public reports of the event of the audit committee meeting and of the private meeting with the internal auditors act as a ceremonial demonstration of the maintenance of high corporate governance standards to an audience external to the company.

5.4 THE ROLE OF THE AUDIT COMMITTEE MEETING: WITHIN THE COMPANY

The meeting event is also performed for an internal audience: it is used by the board of directors as a deterrent, a protection from both fraud and incompetence within the company. Interviewees generally insisted that audit committees would be powerless to prevent calculated fraud (see comments on Robert Maxwell quoted in section 3.7), but incompetence was viewed as an equally serious threat and a belief was expressed that audit committees could combat this by highlighting issues of concern and calling individuals to account. Participants spoke of 'keeping people up to the mark' or 'keeping people on their toes', as, for example, Max Tinker, the finance director at Runic: '…in my experience the audit committee is regarded as an important or a powerful body and so it isn't a question of saying 'I don't feel like appearing' or 'I'll come and busk the answer' because you know you can't. You may be very confident in your own case but you are definitely there appearing a bit like if you like the Houses of Parliament Select committees. However powerful you are certainly in the outside world you have to appear before them... unless you're ill and they'll still have you next time!'

Finance directors and internal auditors referred to 'pulling people in': '..then they'd be called to the chairman of the audit committee and the others would say 'What are we doing about this, it's been raised as an issue now, I don't want to see it there again' - we need to say that we're going to sort it..' (Chris Tracker, Scrimshaw) '..what happens is that most of them [high risk issues identified by internal audit] are taken up by the chief executive and he will follow those up and there have been occasions when management of a particular function have been called to the audit committee to explain ....(Bernard Seaton, Runic) '.. the audit committee for example says periodically 'We're fed up of this, we require the [X division] director to appear before the next meeting and what we want him to address is this, that or the other..'(Max Tinker, Runic)

These comments emphasise the perceived authority of the audit committee within the company. A similar view was expressed by Ken Palmer, an external auditor with considerable experience of audit committees, and the author of several publications offering guidance to audit committee participants. He stated that: 'The audit committee is effective if there are no nasty surprises', a perspective echoed elsewhere in the practitioner literature (see, for example, Warrick and Galloway, 1996)

The concept of the nasty surprise implies evidence of lack of control. Although there may be unexpected changes in an organisation's external environment which are beyond its control, the surprises referred to were seen as evidence of failure of internal control systems. Interviewees observed that it is possible to put elaborate systems in place (balancing cost against value to the company and recognising that all risks cannot be prevented) but that such systems cannot prevent a determined fraudster. Participants' accounts thus focused on the mechanics of audit committee operation, suggesting that the audit committee process itself offered protection against the threat of incompetence and, to a much lesser extent, fraud: ' You assess effectiveness from the perspective of process - does the system work? - and outputs – the lack of surprises, the degree of comfort..'(Ken Palmer) ' The audit committee role is to improve systems and process..' (Bob Cunningham)

The very existence of an audit committee which followed due process was deemed sufficient to achieve this purpose[32]. The prescriptive outcomes of this view are the unsubstantiated accounts of best practice, illustrations of audit committee procedures where no nasty surprises have occurred – yet. Bob Cunningham confessed that he did not know what made an effective audit committee. He suggested that it was 'like the plumbing: as long as it works you don't think about it'.

Here we have a view of the audit committee meeting as a ceremonial performance designed to deter inappropriate behaviour within the company. The calling to account of individuals representing groups within the company is a symbolic display. Chris Tracker, finance director at Scrimshaw commented: 'We need to say that we're going to sort it ' – not 'We need to sort it'. Knowledge that the audit committee exists and can demand reports acts as a deterrent and also as a means of enrolling employees, analogous to Meyer and Rowan's 'logic of confidence' discussed in section 5.5 below.

Chris Tracker's approach to audit committee meetings appeared ambiguous, reflecting a belief that it is necessary for the finance director to 'manage' the meeting but in a way that does not lead to an obviously superficial outcome: this suggests that members are expected to 'perform' and the asking and answering of questions provides this performance, allowing a degree of 'constrained spontaneity': '..you manage the audit committee - basically you make sure that everyone's informed when you go into the meeting, you know where your start point is and your end point is, it doesn't mean managing the discussion before hand. I don't actually say a lot but you know what you don't want is an audit committee that lasts for twenty minutes, right, we've had an audit committee, tick, we've done that for Cadbury..' (Chris Tracker, Scrimshaw)

How performance is managed in the meeting through the asking of questions will be explored in chapter 8.

5.5   THE AUDIT COMMITTEE AS A NETWORK

The performance of the audit committee meeting is directed at audiences both internal and external to the company. It acts as an interessement and enrolment device to draw external parties – and material resources – into the company network and to strengthen that network internally by enrolling company employees through demands for accountability. At a third level, the audit committee is itself a network: its non-executive members are punctualised actors representing the shareholder network[33]. Members have been enrolled by a variety of devices – for example, the enhanced status of serving on the board of a well-known company or working with other directors of high reputation - and are prepared to join together for this public performance, to achieve consensus through compromise and to allow themselves in turn to be represented by the punctualised actor of the audit committee chair who will report to the full board of directors on their behalf. The audit committee network node is then enrolled within the board, strengthening the board network. Simultaneously the participants in audit committee activity are also able to enrol the audit committee to strengthen their own networks. Audit committee participants can use the audit committee as an interessement and enrolment device to achieve their purposes but this is only made possible by the process of establishing the audit committee as a strong network node in its own right. The audit committee meeting and the performance of questioning (discussed in chapter 8) demonstrates this strength and the audit committee thus becomes a 'black box' to be used by participants. The meeting itself thus acts both as an interessement and enrolment device for the company network and as an arena within which its members and other participants can operate to strengthen their own networks.

The ceremonial of the audit committee meeting serves as an interessement and enrolment device on three levels: external to the company, internal to the company and internal to itself. It provides the public symbol external to the company necessary to enrol suppliers of finance and other resources, it acts as a symbol of authority and control within the company, enrolling employees, and it reinforces the links between the members to ensure that as a group they generate the comfort for the board that is passed on to external users of the company's financial statements and ultimately secures the legitimacy of the company.

The audit committee as a network derives its own strength from the skills and experience of its members and from the authoritative support of the Cadbury Code. Meyer and Rowan (1977) observed: 'By designing a formal structure that adheres to the prescriptions of myths in the institutional environment, an organization demonstrates that it is acting on collectively valued purposes in a proper and adequate manner.. The organization becomes, in a word, legitimate, and it uses its legitimacy to strengthen its support and secure its survival' (1977:349) 'The incorporation of structures with high ceremonial value, such as those reflecting the latest expert thinking or those with the most prestige, makes the credit position of an organization more favourable. Loans, donations or investments are more easily obtained.' (1977:351)

Thus, in this analysis, the 'myth' of the Cadbury Code, as a prescription for ensuring higher standards of financial reporting and concomitantly higher standards of corporate governance, leads to the widespread establishment of audit committees in accordance with the Code, used by the companies establishing them as a means of legitimation and access to resources. The means by which legitimacy is established will be explored in subsequent chapters. However, this motive for audit committee establishment was not articulated by interviewees in this study who often appeared to express contradictory views, asserting on the one hand that audit committees could not work in the way envisaged by Cadbury but on the other hand supporting their establishment.

This contradictory approach reflects the concepts of 'espoused theory' and 'theory-in-use' identified by Argyris and Schon (1974): 'When someone is asked how he would behave under certain circumstances, the answer he usually gives is his espoused theory of action for that situation. This is the theory of action to which he gives allegiance and which, upon request, he communicates to others. However, the theory that actually governs his actions is his theory-in-use, which may or may not be compatible with his espoused theory; furthermore, the individual may or may not be aware of the incompatibility of the two theories.' (1974:7)

The 'espoused' theory is the rationale for the establishment of audit committees, despite the lack of evidence that they 'work' as intended in achieving their programmatic purpose: the 'theory-in-use' underpins the ways in which participants make audit committees 'work' to achieve their individual objectives.

Meyer and Rowan noted that the ceremonial practice adopted – in Power's terms, the programmatic solution (Power, 1997) - is not directly linked to the practice within the organization and may indeed conflict with such practice. This divergence echoes the contradiction in interviewees' accounts between the critical view of the audit committee as exemplified in Cadbury, and the appreciation of its practical use. Meyer and Rowan (1977) use the notion of decoupling to explore the gap between the ceremonial and the practical. Decoupling is supported by 'the logic of confidence': '..committed participants engage in informal coordination that, although often formally inappropriate, keeps technical activities running smoothly and avoids public embarrassments. In this sense the confidence and good faith generated by ceremonial action is in no way fraudulent. It may even be the most reasonable way to get participants to make their best efforts in situations that are made problematic by institutionalized myths that are at odds with immediate technical demands' (1977:358-9)

The concept of decoupling offers a partial explanation of how the gap between audit committee rhetoric and practice is managed. For example, how can a committee meeting for approximately two hours three or four times a year adequately exercise the internal control functions envisaged by Cadbury? One might expect the audit committee to have a significant impact on the operation of the internal audit function in fulfilling these requirements. Yet at Hobson plc no internal audit function existed or was thought to be necessary by Michael Tyler, the deputy chairman, despite his assertion that the Hobson audit committee was a Cadbury exemplar. When asked if an internal audit department existed at another company where he chaired the audit committee, Michael Tyler responded: 'I don't know – there may be one.' Other interviewees reported no change in the day-to-day activity of internal audit as a result of audit committee activity: indeed, Bernard Seaton at Runic would have welcomed such evidence of a proactive audit committee. Robin Dunston at Scrimshaw valued the audit committee as an enabling device – 'a lever' – and appreciated the direct access to the board afforded by its existence and reporting requirements but indicated that he spent much time 'educating' audit committee members, 'I'm not sure I've yet got them quite to understand the range of work we cover', and this perspective was shared with Simon Middleton at Glengarry. Although these internal auditors report to the audit committee, there is a clear sense in their accounts of this relationship that in practice that they are 'calling the shots' rather than the committee: on one internal control issue Robin Dunston observed: 'I think we came up with a solution before they asked'. It is possible that closer links between the ceremonial performance of audit committees and the practical implementation of internal audit procedures do exist and/or may develop but within this study a significant decoupling has been identified.

5.6 THE AUDIT COMMITTEE MEETING AS A 'CENTRE OF TRANSLATION': PROBLEMATISATION

Within the audit committee meeting participants are able to problematise issues and use particular features of the meeting process as interessement and enrolment devices to achieve individual objectives.

The use of the audit committee and its activities as a lever was a metaphor used by Robin Dunston, the internal auditor at Scrimshaw: 'In some ways it [the audit committee] is a nuisance – on the other hand, it's another lever I can pull..'

One benefit of audit committee establishment asserted within the literature is the raising of the profile of the internal audit function (see, for example, Charkham, 1989:13) and it was evident that internal auditors interviewed particularly valued audit committee support and sought to be proactive in achieving it, sometimes through 'educating' audit committee members: 'I'm not sure I've yet got them quite to understand the range of work we cover, the sorts of things we come up with and how its progressed in the business and they're almost taking a simplistic view....it's a little more shaded and complicated than I think perhaps they think at the moment. I'm mulling this over – perhaps I need to get the chairman off line and run him through a few audit reports...' (Robin Dunston, Scrimshaw)

One issue raised at Runic, Scrimshaw and Glengarry was the difficulty in establishing the 'control culture' of the acquiring company within a foreign subsidiary and the useful role the audit committee could play in this. At Scrimshaw, Robin Dunston described the problems of introducing the company's approach to controls in foreign subsidiaries, observing that it was difficult for him to go in and tell them 'how to do internal audit': '..the fact that I can translate what they [the audit committee] think into other companies has helped.'

At Runic, Bernard Seaton reported to the audit committee that: '..at [subsidiary company] there had been a refusal to admit access to Corporate Internal Audit. This situation could not be accepted and the matter would be followed through by the [Runic] representative on the [subsidiary company] audit committee. The recent change at managing director level at [subsidiary company] should present a renewed opportunity to resolve this issue.'(Runic audit committee minutes)

Bernard Seaton hoped that the fact that the audit committee had formally recognised the existence of this problem would emphasise its importance to the management of the subsidiary company and allow his team to undertake their normal work.

At Glengarry, Alex Anderson explained: '.. there are certain big issues arising from big reorganisations in other countries.. the audit committee has pushed ....to ensure that management would never lose sight of the fact that those were the very big risk areas. In [subsidiary company] we had a billion pounds invested but didn't have much idea of what was going on so the audit committee could push and push for more efforts by management, however much it might upset the [subsidiary company management], to dig in and try and find out more of what was going on.'

The context of these comments suggests that in this instance the audit committee was perhaps being used to undertake executive responsibilities. Glengarry had passed through a significant crisis some years previously. During the management changes effected to resolve the crisis, Martin Johnson, the current audit committee chair, had been brought in as the company's finance director. He had previously had a high profile career as a finance director and was proud that he had established audit committees long before the publication of the Cadbury Code: 'I've always been a finance director who likes to have a proper structure in place - I formed an audit committee at [company] when I became the first finance director there that they'd ever had...If I was having difficulty in pushing through the control culture they [the audit committee] would take it on board and support it.'

He expressed the belief that the finance director's role was closely linked to that of the audit committee: 'It's sometimes forgotten that the finance director of a big sprawling multinational group himself is actually the most independent person - he's not actually in operations at all, he is effectively the chairman and chief executive's right hand to make sure you keep everybody honest.'

It was clear that he had found it difficult to detach himself from the activities of the finance function, although he claimed that the board supported these close links: 'About that time they also appointed a very young finance director so I was asked to act as a sort of mentor.'

Simon Middleton, the internal auditor, expressed the view that this blurring of role contributed to what he described as the 'rather tense relationship' between Martin Johnson and the company chairman which was played out in audit committee meetings.

The Glengarry stories demonstrate ways in which audit committee participants may seek to 'use' the audit committee as a lever by problematising and drawing attention to specific issues. Although the rhetoric of the audit committee, expressed in Cadbury, offers a picture of an independent group, identifying and pursuing issues autonomously, the audit committee is dependent on finance directors and internal auditors for information and it is unlikely to operate in such detached isolation. However, as the situation at Glengarry illustrates, there may be grey areas where the audit committee may be drawn into executive functions. Audit committee members may be aware of this, as Henry Morton indicated: 'One of the problems there has been with [Runic] is that they are so keen to do the right thing that you could easily find yourself in the situation that you weren't non-executive, that you were executive - where one's been invited into some discussions .. I think at one stage I actually said to [the company chairman] 'I really don't think that I should be on that committee, it sounds a little bit like an executive committee to me' and you can lose your objectivity and you become involved with the decision and what you should be doing is not taking the decision but vetting the decision. It's difficult ground this - one which an accommodating management, wishing to do the right thing, occasionally can go too far in one way I think.'

As audit committees develop, these grey areas may increase. Clearly defined terms of reference may help but there is a sense here that audit committees are being moved on by participants into a different role which may focus less on the issues for which Cadbury so strongly recommended them. This underlines the divergence of participants' views on the appropriate role for the audit committee and renders the assessment of 'effectiveness' even more difficult.

These accounts indicate examples of issues problematised by participants. The network formation which follows successful problematisation is facilitated by a range of potential interessement and enrolment devices, which participants are able to utilise. Such devices include:

- the documentation associated with meetings (agenda, minutes and information supplied to committee members)
- logistical factors such as timing, location, numbers of people present
- 'conventions' of behaviour (Maddick and Pritchard, 1958) such as language (e.g. use of company-specific acronyms) and seating arrangements.

These are the components of the ceremonial of audit committee meetings: they give a structure to the process which both enables the meeting to take place and defines its parameters. They act as constraints on spontaneity. They are all within the control of specific participants. Their use will be explored in detail in chapter 6.

This chapter has examined the role of the audit committee from an ANT perspective, exploring the use of the ceremonial performance of the audit committee meeting as an interessement and enrolment device both outside and inside the company. It has demonstrated that the meeting also acts as a centre of translation, allowing participants to problematise issues. The concept of decoupling has been suggested as an explanation for the gap identified between participants' criticism of the audit committee rhetoric and their support for audit committees in practice. The next chapter identifies further indications of decoupling as it explores the performance *in* the audit committee meeting, examining how participants make use of the ceremonial components of the meeting to strengthen their own networks. These processes of translation make the audit committee 'work' for them, irrespective of achievement of the Cadbury objectives.

Chapter 6
THE CEREMONIAL COMPONENTS OF THE AUDIT COMMITTEE MEETING

In chapter 5 the audit committee meeting was viewed as a centre of translation, an arena for the creation of further networks among audit committee participants, in which the ceremonial components of the meeting are used by participants as interessement and enrolment devices. The ceremonial components of audit committee meetings were categorised into three areas: documentation, logistics and conventions of behaviour. This chapter examines the use of these components in more detail.

6.1   MEETING DOCUMENTS: THE SUPPLY OF INFORMATION

The documentation associated with meetings – agendas, information supplied for discussion at meetings and minutes - is circulated to audit committee members, other participants and the remaining members of the board (who are normally entitled to attend audit committee meetings if they wish). All of these documents may be used as interessement and enrolment devices by participants.

The agenda and minutes have a formal role in the conduct of a committee, giving structure to its proceedings and providing a formal record of its business. The committee's terms of reference will define the scope of its activities at a broad level: the agenda of each meeting constrains the consideration of specific issues within a particular time frame. For example, a very crowded agenda may impose pressures on the committee that limit full debate and this constraint may be used to the advantage of particular participants. The audit committee agenda acts as a vehicle for problematisation. The agenda is formally prepared by the company secretary (usually the secretary to the audit committee) on the basis of discussions with other participants, usually the finance director and the audit committee chair, sometimes also the chief executive, the company chairman and the internal auditor.

At Scrimshaw and Glengarry, the finance directors emphasised a team approach in answer to the question 'Who prepares the agenda for audit committee meetings?' '..really a combination of myself, the secretary - pulling things out of the previous minutes et cetera, and obviously the internal audit manager, he's important, picking up any points between the three of us..' (Chris Tracker) 'The agenda is actually approved by the chairman of the audit committee and normally would be prepared by the group company secretary who attends and would take the minutes of the meeting so he'd prepare the agenda in terms of input to that agenda and then I would put forward what I think should go onto it and the head of group audit would - there are a number of standing items we cover any way and the chairman would review and may add or delete as he thinks appropriate, I mean, all this with discussion with us, do we want to - at the end of the day do we need to talk about this, should it be on ?' (Alex Anderson)

Both Chris and Alex were keen to stress that they did not take sole responsibility for agenda preparation. At Runic, the balanced provision of information was emphasised:

'You can manipulate it [the meeting]- for example, I do the agenda and that's probably the most powerful single tool...I would say that was principally the way that one would control it and the other way is talking to the chairman beforehand, getting your point of view across because people tend to agree with you when you talk to them so you can if you like lead to a conclusion or emphasise one particular point of view. Counter balanced to that I think and in our case it's a pretty powerful counterbalance is that the auditors produce a memorandum to the audit committee which deals with the numbers in the accounts, deals with presentational matters, SSAPs[34] and so on ... although I play a part in that as well and they take that through the chairman and the chief executive before its published. None the less, if they're strong enough that's a parallel source of information going in to the audit committee and it deals with the salient points so ..I can't exclude items because they're there and the auditors are saying 'Look these are the important points' so I can't really belittle them either so, yes, you can manipulate it or control it to some extent but there are checks and balances, at least there are in our case.' (Max Tinker)

The words 'manipulate', 'control' and 'counterbalance' and the phrase 'if they're strong enough' convey a sense of two groups – the executive directors and the external auditors – competing to enrol the audit committee members through the use of information. The complexities of such competition within the audit committee arena are explored in more detail in the case of Runic in chapter 7. While emphasising the independent input of the external auditors, Max Tinker indicated that this input is subject to discussion with company executives before it is presented to the audit committee. Indeed, he highlighted the importance of such interaction in the development of the written information: '..people tend to agree with you when you talk to them so you can if you like lead to a conclusion or emphasise one particular point of view'.

A similar procedure was outlined by Alex Anderson at Glengarry: '..the auditors wouldn't submit a paper without making sure that the facts in it have been agreed by us, otherwise you get into dreadful trouble about things that seem totally irrelevant as far as the directors are concerned, but you've got to have accurate information. But there's no stopping people asking questions or making particular points so you know they are quite good from that point of view ..'

Alex did not provide an illustration of the 'dreadful trouble' that was avoided through this process. The final sentence of this extract seems to indicate a certain defensiveness: all the information provided to the committee has been approved by the information 'gatekeepers' – who thus constitute an obligatory passage point – so that the important direct link envisaged by Cadbury between the audit committee and the external auditors has been circumvented. However, Alex indicated that committee members are still able to question the information providers. The role played by the questioning procedure is discussed more extensively in chapter 8.

Chris Tracker was emphatic about the objectivity of the information supplied: 'I also ensure that the information that's available is factually correct and not pruned so I don't go around saying we can't talk about that, take that out or anything like that.. basically you make sure that everyone's informed when you go into the meeting..'

These accounts emphasise the objectivity and accuracy of the information supplied to the audit committee and a balanced approach representing all points of view. However, the provision of information does not guarantee that committee members will use it appropriately. The actual use made of this written information was not made clear by interviewees, although they expressed the view that NEDs were required to absorb a great deal, particularly the audit committee chair. Max Tinker suggested that members might not make very effective use of the written information supplied: '..other members of the audit committee probably just turn up on the day having leafed through the papers.'

As Henry Morton pointed out:

'.. there's a lot of reading to be done before, particularly in Runic I think because some of the issues are fairly complex, complex both from the financial angle in terms of currencies, that sort of thing, and in understanding some of the technicalities and the industry, I mean a non exec can never really understand the real intricacies of the industry, all he can do is to get, you know, a general picture .... it requires quite a lot of deep study to understand. Even then you know what you hope you understand and you remember until the next audit committee meeting and then you find yourself doing the homework all over again - very difficult to retain it when you sort of come at it from time to time rather than live with it continuously... there is an accumulation of knowledge from each board meeting of course.'

Henry's account supports the argument for continuity of audit committee membership achieved through lengthy service, as opposed to the position taken by commentators such as PIRC[35] who argue that long service compromises independence. This is discussed further in chapter 8.

Interviewees emphasised the importance of having one audit committee member with a financial background who could interpret the more technical areas: 'You also need someone who is frankly the sort of person who will read all the papers very carefully, you know there's no doubt that the finance guy will read the detailed notes to the accounts and think through the implications and connotations of what's said in a way that's different to somebody who hasn't got that finance background' (Alex Anderson)

Information provided for discussion at the meeting is usually extensive.

'They don't tend to complain about lack of information, we have executive committees about twenty times a year as well as the board meetings and they get all the papers for those....what's interesting I find is that ... every meeting I try to cut it down so they don't have too much and they always seem to want more and more, the non-execs, and that's all about the control issues, the non-execs needing to realise what their responsibilities are ..we do a management summary which has an appendix which is all about all the detail behind, which had to be done to build it up anyway, for internal distribution - once it has gone through the committee I can send it round to the executive directors so that they could then see what was going on in their respective areas - so the management summary simply went out with 'If you like, a more detailed summary is available' and all of them asked for it.' (Chris Tracker at Scrimshaw) 'I suppose with us there's probably too much information in this business and the history you know following [the company crisis] was to produce huge great books to make sure every number could be reconciled every which way.... we're not short of information, we do produce a lot of quite lengthy reports certainly in terms of the financial statements, there is a lot of information.' (Alex Anderson)

These comments suggest that audit committee members derive some comfort from the volume and extent of the information supplied. Max Tinker explained how his experience as a non-executive director had influenced the quality of information provided at Runic: 'I actually think if you have a non executive position it helps because you can see it from the other side - you get a different perspective and see what your own non execs are doing...I've tended to give more of the argument rather than just sort of state what it is we're looking to do. Perhaps a large investment or something so 'Here's the investment, the recommendation is that we go ahead', that's fine if you know the background to it and you've probably argued a couple of papers internally but for a non exec there's a big gap in the middle which is 'Well, tell us the options, where's the calculations?' and so on, so it's had that sort of effect on me. It may not be a wholly desirable effect for the non exec because it means more and more paper.'

Max's experience thus helped him to make more effective use of information as an enrolment device at Runic.

Minutes of audit committee meetings are formally prepared by the company secretary but the finance director often has considerable influence: 'I also clear the minutes although the secretary of the company is the secretary and clears the minutes with the chairman - none the less, I intervene partly to see that they're factual because you know it's hard work writing minutes and, if you're not financial, it's even harder work doing audit committee minutes..'(Max Tinker)

Max's considerate assistance for the company secretary would presumably also allow him the opportunity for judicious amendment where he believed it to be necessary.

The minutes are the main channel of report to the main board. Interviewees reported that recommendations were likely to be accepted with little comment: board members are generally happy to delegate the issues that form the audit committee's terms of reference. Max Tinker commented: 'People get bored and drift off frankly and sort of you know essentially I think people would say 'Why the hell don't we leave this to the members of the board who know what it's all about'.

Alex Anderson observed: '..you can't spend board meetings going through stuff the audit committee has already been through.' - although the issue at Runic which is examined in detail in the next chapter did lead to extensive board discussion.

This contrasts with the findings of Samuels et al (1996) who observed in their study of the role of NEDs after Cadbury that '..a number of main board executive directors now felt they were being by-passed on audit matters' (1996:12) However, interviewees in this study indicated that members of the board rarely exercise their option to attend audit committee meetings. At Scrimshaw, Chris Tracker observed: '..they tend to only attend when they're invited ... they don't tend to come along - they see the non-execs at the board and if they've got any issues - subsequent discussions, they can raise them there.'

These accounts indicate that, where the 'gatekeeper' who controls access to the information needed for audit committee deliberation is also influential in preparing the agenda and the minutes, that individual can then ·become an obligatory passage point, with the opportunity of enrolling audit committee participants to achieve the objectives problematised. The power of the finance director as the usual gatekeeper is very significant, although balanced to some extent by external auditors' reports and commentaries, the questioning role of the non-executive audit committee members (discussed further in chapter 8) and the 'strength of character' of the chairman, as indicated by Max Tinker: '... it depends upon the strength of the chairman of the audit committee - by and large, because audit committees are comprised of non executive directors and they turn up on the day and use their knowledge and background, if you like, rather than perhaps having played a big role in between audit committee meetings, the chairman of the audit committee should, I think, be more active and hence talk to the finance director and so on, so, you know, it depends who is the stronger character really..'

Documented meeting information is thus extensive (possibly leading to information overload, possibly not read in detail by all audit committee members) and controlled by the finance director and other participants (even the material provided by the external auditor is discussed beforehand with the information 'gatekeepers'). It may be quite technical and require interpretation by a finance expert. There is an expectation that this written information will be explored and possibly extended by audit committee members through questioning. The skills and personal qualities of the NEDs are clearly crucial – they need to be able to interpret the information, identify areas where it is inadequate or needs further explanation, and seek to fill such gaps through intelligent questioning, understanding the adequacy of the responses.[36]

The practical value of such information as support for rational argument is also augmented by its symbolic nature. Feldman and March (1981) discussed the symbolic use of information in organisations. They observed: 'The gathering of information provides a ritualistic assurance that appropriate attitudes about decision making exist. Within such a scenario of performance, information is not simply a basis for action. It is a representation of competence and a reaffirmation of social virtue. Command of information and information sources enhances perceived competence and inspires confidence' (1981:177)

There is certainly a sense in interviewees' accounts that audit committee members derive reassurance from the provision of extensive information: the role of this 'ritualistic assurance' will be further explored in chapters 8 and 9.

6.2   MEETING LOGISTICS

The setting for the audit committee meetings in the companies in this study was normally the board room or an equivalent. In some cases numbers attending may be significant. At Harrier, for example, Roy Milford described the logistical problems of large numbers of attendees:
'... the room where we are sitting - this room isn't big enough for our audit committee - we open it up - we bring that table in there which is the same as these two so we have three of these tables...so we have in the room five auditors, three non -execs, two company secretaries, two from finance, the poor creatures who are being done over, Keith [his deputy] and me, three internal auditors and JJ [Jeremy James, deputy chairman]..[so] we need a big room! That was who came to the last audit committee meeting - one of the internal auditors won't come again so we're down to two, so we'll be down to fifteen, the company secretary I think we can stop coming so we'll be

down to fourteen - it's quite impossible to see how to reduce it from there....
When I've suggested to [the audit committee chair] in the nicest possible
way that we've only got to tell a couple of these people not to come and they
won't, she won't hear of it - she thinks it's me being devious and trying to
keep someone out..'

The number attending may be a constraint on audit committee
activities but is, to some extent, within the control of the audit committee
chairman. The comment quoted above indicates that at Harrier, the chairman
did not agree to the finance director's suggestion of reducing the numbers
attending: although Roy Milford expressed the view that she saw these
numbers as some sort of protection against possible manipulation by him, it
is possible that the large number attending may in fact act to the advantage
of the finance director. Bailey (1977) discussed the effect on committee
behaviour of large numbers: he noted that effective operation may be limited
by physical constraints of space, by the difficulty of organising sensible
debate and compromise among a large number and by the need to simplify
information. He observed that: '..as you multiply the numbers present, so
also you multiply the chances of including stupid people, opinionated
people, unreasonable people and destructive people.'(1977:63)

He also noted that 'by increasing the size you increase temptation to
pay attention to an audience'(1977:63) - participants may be tempted to
'play to the gallery'. Conversely, the size of the group could be intimidating
to someone wishing to raise controversial issues. At Harrier, the finance
director effectively controlled the agenda, the minutes and the information
provided to the committee, exercising considerable influence. The audit
committee chair lived in New York, flying in for board meetings: Roy
Milford explained that he usually met her in a car at Heathrow and briefed
her on the journey into London. Lack of frequent communication with the
audit committee chair might however be a handicap in terms of
interessement and enrolment. Max Tinker pointed out the advantages of:
'...talking to the chairman beforehand, getting your point of view across
because people tend to agree with you when you talk to them so you can if
you like lead to a conclusion or emphasise one particular point of view.'

Where audit committees had been established for a longer period of
time, interviewees reported regular contact with the audit committee chair,
as at Glengarry:
'[Martin] certainly puts in a lot of time and is available for us to consult
outside audit committee meetings anyway so if there are things that we're

particularly concerned about we'd actually speak to him...we have operations in a number of countries with soft currencies, you know, just thinking through how we manage our exposures in those countries, I mean, so there's actually been quite a lot of correspondence with him, either on the phone or in writing on exactly what we ought to do in those areas so that's an example of where we've had the benefit of his input outside the formal audit committee. We always have meetings ahead of audit committee meetings to take him through the papers and to brief him on what the issues are and to give him the opportunity to ask questions about issues he would want to raise outside - the very detailed technical questions..' (Alex Anderson)

As previously noted, Martin Johnson was perhaps more closely involved in such deliberations than would normally be the case. There is however no doubt that the channels of communication between audit committee participants play a central part in the provision and use of information by the committee and this supplements the written documentation which may indeed be ceremonial in format and presentation.

Another important logistical factor relates to the timing of the audit committee meeting in relation to the main board meeting. The difficulties of synchronising the diaries of busy people suggest that the most practical time for the audit committee to meet is immediately before the main board meeting - as Bob Cunningham, put it: 'The audit committee meeting is adjacent to the main board meeting because the chaps are there'. However, in some companies, this was found to be an unacceptable constraint. Chris Tracker described changes made at Scrimshaw:

'... [audit committee meetings] always take place a few days before so that if there are any issues they can be picked up and dealt with before the main board meeting. To be honest when I started here the audit committee chair then, because he was extremely busy - one of these active non execs with lots of appointments - he used to quite like having it in the morning like nine o'clock, the board starts at ten, something like that, but after about two years we began to realise that it was totally impractical, we didn't get the assurance that we needed if there were issues - I couldn't rush out in two minutes and get the answer. So now you know they tend to be on - it depends on the time and what it is - if it's the year end that you're worried about or the half year, you can't have it weeks before because you haven't got the results to look at, you know, so they tend to be Monday, I mean the next one's Monday with the board on Thursday, but it depends on diaries as much as anything..'

At Glengarry, however, Alex Anderson reported: '[the audit committee] meeting tends to happen on the evening before the main board though that's not always the case. Broadly what we have is three definite meetings per year then there's the fourth if necessary in December and they're normally timed at the convenience of the non executives and it so happens that the evening before the main board is fairly convenient.'

The lack of a time gap was not perceived as a problem and he explained how unresolved audit committee issues would be dealt with: '..the chairman of the audit committee reports to the board on matters discussed at the audit committee meeting and he would clearly report that there was a particular subject that, you know, he'd obviously explain the background et cetera and then say 'This is what action is going to be taken in respect of that item, I'll report further whenever'..'

Max Tinker commented on the Runic practice of leaving a gap of several days between the two meetings:
'From our point of view within the company it's advantageous - first of all, if there are changes and there might be a change for example to the dividend recommendation, so if there are changes and there's often changes in the drafting not necessarily in the numbers or the notes but in the chairman's report so it enables us to print those and get a book proof to the board if it's the finals anyway so really it's giving us a little gap. Also it enables us to produce the minutes so that the full board have the minutes of the audit committee meeting and the chairman of the audit committee time to think what he's going to report. Now all those things are possible in 24 hours or overnight but they're more comfortable [when there is a gap] ...[When the board meeting immediately follows the audit committee meeting] that has the advantage that everything's fresh in your mind and you can talk about it and so on but it is under pressure, there's no doubt and more pre-preparation is therefore necessary. And something like the case I was talking about, the contingent liabilities treatment or presentation[37], really I mean we'd just have regurgitated the same arguments if the one meeting had followed the other very quickly whereas we were able to go away and to produce new arguments, or arguments we'd forgotten anyway!'

A time gap thus works to the advantage of participants providing information. However, audit committee members and chairs interviewed did not comment on this.

Collier (1992:81) observed that the average audit committee meets for a total of seven hours each year. Given the range of activities the committee is expected to undertake, it is clear that much important activity must take place outside the meeting and that the meeting itself must be tightly structured to ensure that all business is attended to. At Glengarry, Alex Anderson outlined the year:

'...we've got meetings in March, May, September and there may or may not be one in December. The March one would be primarily about the year end results, May would be about internal controls - things like control over pension funds and ...we would discuss the delegation of authorities and consider whether any changes were necessary and then September - internal control would be primarily - there'd be the [external auditor] internal control report ...and final [external audit] fees - September would be audit strategy ... last time round we actually did group audit plans and obviously the interim statement and possibly accounting developments though if we know we're going to have a meeting in December we do that then as well .. and accounting developments would include any new financial reporting standards, anything of relevance from the Auditing Practices Board of that sort of nature and we'd also pick up if we were looking to change a particular accounting policy which is unlikely, but if circumstances had changed, we'd cover that at that stage and get audit committee approval, so those are the key areas.'

This is a significant amount of business and, in a year when a number of accounting and/or auditing standards might be issued, audit committee members would be required to assimilate a daunting amount of information.

The structure and timing of meetings form part of the ceremonial of audit committee meetings and are set by participants: they can operate to the advantage of particular individuals or groups. They may inhibit spontaneity: despite the insistence of interviewees on the atmosphere of open discussion with the opportunity for members to ask questions, such questioning is only enabled within specific constraints. As Moore and Myerhoff (1977) observed: 'Ritual discourages inquiry, not only because it presents its material authoritatively, as axiomatic. It is itself a message stated in a form to render it unverifiable, separate from standards of truth and falsity... ..formality as such often conveys an element of presented certainty.' (1977:22)

6.3   CONVENTIONS OF BEHAVIOUR

The ceremonial nature of meetings is further underscored by behavioural conventions adopted by those present. Messages about the role and status of participants are conveyed through seating arrangements, the use of language and even dress code: Robin Dunston described the Scrimshaw audit committee meeting as 'jackets on rather than jackets off, if you know what I mean.' Such messages are used as interessement and enrolment devices, emphasising the situation of individuals as part of particular network groupings.

Maddick and Pritchard (1958,1959) studied local government committees and asserted that: 'Like any other committee, they need a lead, and it makes a great deal of difference who gives this lead.[38] This depends to some extent on personalities but it depends chiefly on conventions, which affect the part played by chairman, other members of committees, and officers.'(1958:146)

Their study revealed considerable differences in practice among local government committees which they ascribed to the adoption of conventions influenced by local habit and characteristics: they were unable to generalise about such patterns but emphasised the controlling influence of local conventions in committee behaviour, noting for example that: '..a newly appointed officer will tend to find a conventional code has been woven around his position. The deviant officer is likely to succumb to the pressure of custom..' (1959:139)

Similarly, Bailey (1983) commented on the integration of a new member into a committee, noting that his/her behaviour was likely to exhibit either an apologetic approach, acknowledging a lack of familiarity with the committee's conventions, or an assertive approach demonstrating that the newcomer is a force to be reckoned with. Conventions of behaviour may be communicated in different ways according to the committee's stage of development. Bailey divided the life of a committee into three periods - immaturity, adulthood and senility - and suggested that communication 'codes' differ in each period. In an immature committee: '..messages are likely to be simple, unqualified and emphatically delivered. They convey attitudes and feelings about people and things rather than information or plans to get work done.' (1983:104)

The communication process becomes more refined during the 'adult' period, although Bailey observed that this very refinement contributes to a certain amount of ambiguity about messages conveyed: however, his view was that 'a committee that has at its disposal a well-developed code is usually better able than an immature committee to deal with real problems.' (1983:104) The final senile stage is characterised by such extensive familiarity among members that they: 'have got to know each other so well that they think they can read each other's mind; that it has all been seen and done before anyway; that nothing is new, and therefore there is no point in communicating with an external world.'(1983:104)[39]

While this continuum of development seems intuitively appropriate, Bailey noted that every committee may not advance through these stages and also that the behaviours of each stage may be exhibited in the same committee at the same time.

The 'senile' stage is reached when the sophisticated code itself becomes a symbol to the members of the committee. Committee 'ineffectiveness' is thus associated with the immature and senile stages of development. The immature committee is constrained by its simple code and what Bailey described as 'emotional posturing' - its main function is limited to 'letting off steam'. The senile committee is similarly locked into 'overcoding': the code itself has become a ritual and the committee is unable to respond to external influences. Bailey's analysis suggests that ritual is associated with the senile stage of committee development where the committee becomes completely introverted: 'The committee meetings become ritual performances; no new kinds of information are accepted because the received wisdom comprises all that is needed; and the committee is incapable of doing anything that it has not done before.' (1983:115-6)

However this study argues that the ritual of the committee forms part of the communication that Bailey calls 'codes', rather than a demonstration of the level of code used by the committee.

Many companies have their own internal language – acronyms which provide a convenient linguistic shorthand and are also impenetrable to outsiders. Robin Dunston observed that this reflected an aspect of the Scrimshaw culture, a 'need to keep out the outsiders, once you understand you must be an insider by definition'. Scrimshaw is still significantly controlled by members of its founding family, one of whom had been an executive director some fifteen years previously and had recently returned to the board as a non-executive. Robin described how, at the first audit committee meeting the new NED attended, he had asked for an explanation of all the acronyms currently in use – the other audit committee members had appeared to be palpably relieved, having never dared to ask. Robin also observed that at the Scrimshaw audit committee meetings, the chairman was always addressed as 'Chairman', even by those who would normally use his first name outside the meeting, and that everyone was referred to by their initials where, again, first names would be used outside the meeting.

Seating arrangements form another ceremonial component. Questions about seating patterns were greeted with surprise by most interviewees who had clearly never given this much conscious thought [40]. As noted in chapter 3, such questions sometimes elicited differing answers from those attending the same meetings. At Glengarry, Alex Anderson gave a detailed account, drawing diagrams: 'Do people always sit in the same places? I suppose no, though it's changed over the last two years. The chairman would sit - I mean it's a long oblong table so the chairman would tend to sit in the seat that the chairman of any meeting tends to sit in, half way down one side, back to the wall actually - I'll draw it for you.' but Martin Johnson, the audit committee chair, expressed surprise at the question and wanted an explanation of its relevance before answering with a sketchy description which did not match that of Alex.

Max Tinker described the potential for deliberate confusion of roles in a meeting where additional attendees may well outnumber 'official' committee members:

'it's very interesting .. here we had a chairman who … believed he was - and to a large extent he was - the only guy who knew about the outside world, the City and so on - the rest of the board had grown up in [Runic] …… so he would not really allow anybody to provide information outside the company, was very cautious about what information was provided and chaired the audit committee… so here was the chairman, executive, chairing the audit committee, and it was quite clear that the finance director wasn't on the audit committee but it was not quite clear who was attending and who was actually on the committee… he then became non executive and now felt that he was fully able to chair the audit committee and did, but because he was chairman of the board and the non execs owed their positions to him basically and some of them for quite a long time, he dominated the meetings. He then left and the guy who had been chief executive took over as chairman and it's quite interesting to see where he sits - he knows he's not on the audit committee but he sits on the side of the table where the audit committee are and, just to confuse matters, we've now got one member of the audit committee who sits on the other side so it's very much a round table discussion rather than a them and us, but it is very definitely them and us and properly so in my view, but it's quite interesting, questions come from all sorts of angles instead of just from across the table..'

Max, as a relative newcomer to the meetings, was clearly sensitive to the signals sent by the seating arrangements and changes that he had noticed. Henry Morton's account of the previous chairman and his own relationship with him was frank: '.. he used to chair it [the audit committee], which was I suppose a little bit naughty but I knew [him] quite well and I think when he brought me in, he started the audit committee and although he chaired it I think he did look to me to advise him, we were very close so I think it worked alright but of course with the chairman of the company also being chairman of the audit committee some things could be steam-rollered through if one has to honest about it..' but Henry indicated that the seating arrangements were unchanging, simply a matter of long-standing habit:
' [it's] a ritual at Runic - the chairman of the meeting always sits with his back to the window right in the middle there, and the chief executive if he's attending always sits dead opposite him and the finance director to his right and the company secretary to his left and so that rule in the broadest possible sense is followed at the [audit committee] meetings - I just edge along and go into the chairman's seat very tentatively[41] but otherwise people sit where they normally sit [at main board meetings]. We try and avoid an adversarial situation where the executives are sitting over there you know because it isn't adversarial actually but [the chairman of the company] is there, [the chief executive] is there and Max is there of course.'

Henry did not indicate how the avoidance of an adversarial situation was implemented: this would certainly require a recognition among those involved of the subtle messages sent out by seating arrangements. No such concerns were expressed at Scrimshaw: 'We have an oval board room table and - no, the chairman tends to sit in different places. We tend to have if you like internal people one side of this sort of curve, executives, non execs and internal audit and then the auditors the other side.' (Chris Tracker)

At Harrier, Roy Milford's main concern (see section 2 above) was fitting all those attending into the room, although he had observed a fairly regular seating pattern, again reflecting the main board meeting pattern.

To some extent, observations about seating arrangements seemed to be linked to status at the meeting: those attending the meeting who were not committee members – finance directors and internal auditors, for example - seemed more likely to observe in a detached way and provide apparently detailed description, while some audit committee chairmen replied that they had never noticed, or dismissed the question as an irrelevance. The chair of a meeting may have less time to observe such detail, or may be very conscious of – even in control of - the messages sent by seating arrangements but not wish to indicate this in his responses. The Runic stories were the clearest indication that seating arrangements may be used to influence committee proceedings but neither Bernard Seaton nor Ronald Roberts demonstrated any awareness of this in their stories of the same meetings.

6.4   CEREMONIAL COMPONENTS AS AN INDICATION OF AUDIT COMMITTEE EVOLUTION

The characteristics of these ceremonial components permit a basic classification of audit committee types which maps on to a similar continuum to that proposed by Bailey through his analysis of communication codes, discussed in the previous section. Audit committees may be characterised as either *active* or *passive*.[42] Thus an *active* audit committee would probably have been established pre-Cadbury, have developed its own clearly stated terms of reference, have well-established channels of communication among participants and would meet sufficiently in advance of the main board meeting to be able to deal with complex issues before reporting to the full board. An *active* audit committee would demonstrate a questioning approach, displayed in the tenor of meetings, the level and type of communication among members outside meetings, requests for information and recommendations to the main board. A *passive* audit committee would probably have been established in response to Cadbury, using the specimen terms of reference provided by Cadbury, and conduct relatively brief meetings immediately prior to the main board meeting. A *passive* committee would display a more submissive nature, content to be fed information at meetings of a more overtly managed character. Thus the 'ineffective' audit committees described by interviewees in section 5.1 would be characterised as passive. The evolution of audit committees along this continuum is explored in more detail in Spira (1998).

The distinction between *active* and *passive* may also be linked to Meyer and Rowan's concept of decoupling. Thus a *passive* audit committee would be part of the ceremonial framework and would not be a part of the substantive company activity. In *active* mode, the audit committee appears to move closer to the Cadbury exemplar and an integration of the programmatic and the technical. However, in both modes the ceremonial of audit committee performance both *of* and *in* meetings is of vital importance for external legitimation and internal authority and the ceremonial components continue to act as interessement and enrolment devices enabling participants to mobilise resources strengthen networks to achieve their own objectives within the audit committee arena.

This chapter has explored the ways in which audit committee participants use the ceremonial components of audit committee meetings – documentation, logistics and conventions of behaviour – as interessement and enrolment devices to strengthen networks around the audit committee and to achieve their objectives. The next chapter identifies the emphasis in participants' stories on consensus and demonstrates the formation and re-formation of networks and their role in the achievement of consensus through an analysis of a specific issue which arose at Runic plc.

Chapter 7:
CONTENTION AND CONSENSUS

The previous chapter examined the use of 'ceremonial components' of audit committee meetings as interessement and enrolment devices by participants seeking to strengthen networks. In this chapter, the process of network formation and mobilisation is illustrated through an ANT analysis of the handling of a contentious issue at Runic. This reveals varying models of relationships among audit committee participants and highlights the shifting and fragmentary nature of the networks which form around the audit committee. Participants' emphasis on consensus as opposed to contention is explored and the importance of the achievement of consensus from an individual and an organisational perspective is discussed.

7.1 'LOOKING FOR TROUBLE': CONTENTIOUS ISSUES

The concept of translation provides an appropriate framework for analysing the ways in which audit committees operate because it recognises the dynamic nature of the networks which connect audit committee participants both within the specific areas of audit committee activity and among the wider networks within which audit committee activity is located. By identifying 'moments of translation' (Callon, 1986) and observing the sources of problematisation, the means by which interessement and enrolment are effected and the outcomes of mobilisation, we are able to see how networks form and re-form in response to the further problematisations of contested positions.

To highlight these processes, 'contentious issues' were selected as a focus of discussion. Contentious issues are here defined as issues on which differing opinions are held by audit committee participants, for which resolution must be achieved by some form of negotiation. The emphasis on conflict and contention in ANT studies was noted in chapter 4: this linked to the metaphor of surprise and ambush observed in participants' accounts and prevalent in both the academic and the practitioner literature on audit committees, such as this US example: 'At the core of effective governance is the control environment or culture of each enterprise. Culture is protected and nourished by oversight activities that demand extraordinary strength to ward off the multitude of threats encountered every day...While the spectacular surprises often involve threats like fraud, employee misconduct or errors of commission, governance control failures can span a range of activities from uninformed strategic decisions to inadequate actions taken to solve problems. A defensive strategy includes effective oversight. When threats penetrate all the defences, the perils to the enterprise can be devastating.'(Warrick and Galloway, 1996:1)

An image of the audit committee as an arena for resolving contentious issues may also be perceived in Cadbury: 'Its sponsors were concerned at the perceived low level of confidence both in financial reporting and in the ability of auditors to provide the safeguards which users of company reports sought and expected.' - and one of the underlying factors was identified as: '..competitive pressures both on companies and on auditors which made it difficult for auditors to stand up to demanding boards.'(Cadbury Committee, 1992:14)

The role of the audit committee is seen as central in raising confidence: 'Shareholders look to the audit committee to ensure that the relationship between the auditors and management remains objective and that the auditors are able to put their views in the event of any difference of opinion with management.' (Cadbury Committee, 1992:38)

The role of the audit committee in dispute resolution is also explored in the academic literature. Knapp (1987) discussed the role of the audit committee in the resolution of auditor-management conflict: he concluded that audit committees tend to support auditors in disputes with management but suggested that this was related to the background of audit committee members, with corporate managers tending to be more supportive of auditors than audit committee members from other backgrounds. He also observed that the nature of the dispute was relevant: 'Audit committee members were less likely to support the auditor when the focal issue of a dispute was not the subject of objective technical standards.' (1987:586)

A further factor was the financial health of the company: 'Audit committee members tend to be less supportive of the auditor when the auditee is in strong financial condition.'(1987:586)

Beattie et al (2000) examined interactions between auditors and directors; they distinguished *discussion* from *negotiation* and observed that: 'Audit committees generally reduce the level of negotiation and increase the level of discussion, suggesting that the overall degree of confrontation declines.' (2000:178)

Previous research thus supports the notion of the audit committee as an arena where contentious issues may be explored before referral to the main board but this is not entirely consistent with the views expressed by participants interviewed in this study. Without exception, interviewees preferred to shift the focus from contention to consensus, effectively rejecting my own problematisation. It was repeatedly suggested by interviewees that questions exploring potential areas of contention were erroneously focused. The possibility of conflict arising from the NED role of monitoring fellow directors was minimised and glossed over. Bob Cunningham was emphatic: 'You join a board because you are in sympathy with the aims of the business and the people running it – you're not looking for trouble.'

This perspective reinforces the image of a united band of audit committee participants seeking to defend shareholders interests against the twin threats of fraud and incompetence, confirming the Cadbury picture. It also allows interviewees to present themselves as reasonable individuals, working as part of a team, although the emphasis on positive consensual outcomes contrasts with the accounts provided of audit committee inadequacy failure noted in section 5.1. Further issues arising from this re-problematisation by interviewees are discussed in section 7.6 below where the importance and role of consensus is assessed.

Contentious issues were viewed by interviewees as unusual. Most interviewees had initial difficulty in identifying examples: with hindsight, they apparently viewed audit committee activity as a seamless and unbroken process, with no specific 'skirmishes' (Singleton and Michael,1993). Max Tinker's comment was typical: 'By and large we don't have many disagreements here. We certainly don't have disagreements on things that people would go to the post for..'

When offered hypothetical examples of issues that might be experienced as contentious, such as accounting policy changes, some participants explained that such matters would be dealt with at an informal level before developing into a contentious situation. The locus of discussion would not be the audit committee meeting. Accounting policies were negotiable although negotiation would normally be conducted outside formal audit committee meetings: 'We haven't yet had a disagreement between management and the external auditors that's needed to go to the audit committee but I don't think you'd expect to get in that sort of state.' (Chris Tracker, Scrimshaw)

At Hobson, Michael Tyler claimed initially that he did not understand the concept of a contentious issue and finally asserted that if any did arise, they would be dealt with before the audit committee met since 'no one would wish them to be debated at length in the audit committee.' He used the expressions 'meeting of minds' and 'compromise' frequently but dismissed the idea of any distinction between formal and informal communication among board members, asserting that 'dialogue is continuous – the members of a board are colleagues working to achieve the objectives of the company'. In the context of Hobson plc, a company chaired and aggressively led by a dynamic and entrepreneurial individual of international repute, Michael's emphasis on the board as team was considerably at variance with the public image of the company.

Clearly, perspectives differ: one person's 'dispute' may be another person's 'reasoned debate':

'.. it depends what you mean by a dispute.. at the end of last year, for example, there was a particular item in the accounts that we decided to treat in one particular way - the auditors said the way we're treating it is perfectly acceptable but there was another way that they, on balance, would prefer. There was a discussion about it and in the end we went down the road that we suggested, so I mean you could call that a dispute but actually I would call it raising an issue and having it properly debated and resolved ......in the paper I wrote for the audit committee I made it quite clear that there were two ways of dealing with this and that we had chosen a particular way for particular reasons, there was no question of ducking the issue with the audit committee by not telling them or presenting the thing in a balanced way.' (Alex Anderson, Glengarry)

This 'balanced presentation' is in itself an enrolment device: there is little scope for audit committee meetings to open up the debate in the context of the time available (at Glengarry, the audit committee normally meets on the evening prior to the main board meeting) and the apparent rationality of the arguments presented may well inhibit debate.

There were, however, undeniable areas of tension. Such areas could be declared 'off limits' through established conventions of behaviour. For example, Roy Milford was horrified at the prospect of the Harrier audit committee insisting on changes to the financial reports: '..what they tend not to do, thankfully, is say the accounts should change.. they're not accountants and in the end I would find that more than just painful..'

He amplified the last sentence by adding that ' the audit committee should back me or sack me'.

More frequently, participants indicated that debate would take place outside the audit committee meetings: the meetings would confirm that consensus had been achieved and allow the audit committee chairman to report this to the main board. '..we've had lots of discussions about things like, you know, presentation, directors' emolument presentation, and things like that, but we've had those internally with the external auditors and we've always reached again agreement and I've then presented it in effect to the audit committee saying 'This is what we're planning to do'..' (Chris Tracker, Scrimshaw)

'We do strive to try and make sure we resolve issues before they get to the audit committee...in some cases there's a lot of debate before the committee meeting...I've been in situations where there have been issues which are arising and although you might not directly meet with members of the audit committee, everyone agrees that everyone ought to talk to everybody a lot before we get to the audit committee and to make sure that everybody knows where everyone's coming from because I mean purely because it saves such a lot of time..' (Ronald Roberts, Runic/XYZ)

Such examples of substantive activity taking place outside the meeting provide further evidence for the existence of decoupling, as noted in section 5.5.

In other situations, a level of 'constrained dissension' demonstrated through questioning acts as a confirming device and is tolerated and indeed turned to advantage by participants, using it for interessement/enrolment. This is illustrated in the discussion of consensus achievement at Runic which follows.

Bailey (1965) explored the distinctions between committees which arrive at decisions on the basis of consensus and those which vote, grounding his observations in his experience of Indian village councils and of university committees. He examined the concept of consensus, suggesting that it has considerable importance in decisions in communities where individuals have multiple interactions with the same group of people and would be unable to conduct their daily business if disagreement was widespread. However, he distinguished between the expression or suppression of dispute and degrees of readiness to compromise, observing that: 'An avoidance of open dispute does not necessarily mean a readiness to compromise and to seek for unanimity; nor does plain speaking, even abuse, automatically and always indicate intransigence.' (1965:8)

Avoidance of open dispute may allow individuals to demonstrate their own reasonableness and understanding of committee etiquette. However, in situations where conflict will impede future action at the expense of all concerned, Bailey suggested that compromise will be sought.

However, participants' accounts of audit committee activity do not focus on decision-making: the role of the audit committee is couched in reactive terms. The duties outlined in the specimen terms of reference included in Cadbury use the words 'consider', 'discuss' and 'review' (Cadbury Committee, 1992:93) The outcomes of such activities are limited to requests for information and referral to the main board: the specimen terms of reference give the committee authority only to investigate relevant matters and to seek external professional advice. Within this framework, where does contention arise and how and why is it resolved into consensus? These questions are explored through an examination of a specific issue of contention which arose at Runic. Tracing the 'moments of translation' in this episode illustrates the formation and re-formation of networks among audit committee participants and the use of interessement and enrolment devices: the participants' views of the importance of consensus achievement are also highlighted, offering insight into the use of consensus itself as an interessement/enrolment device, a further network resource.[43]

7.2 'HOW MUCH SHOULD WE TELL THEM?': THE PROBLEM OF DISCLOSURE

At the core of controversy about financial reporting is the issue of disclosure. The shift in the approach to financial reporting from stewardship to decision-making (noted in chapter 1) has reinforced the view that increased disclosure of information is beneficial for users of financial statements. The extent of information disclosed has increased substantially in the last thirty years: the accounting standard setting regime has had considerable success in this area. However, problematic areas remain. Can the information be understood by users? Is it relevant to users' needs? The balance between satisfying the information needs of users at a reasonable cost while maintaining commercial secrecy is a delicate one which fundamentally influences the selection of accounting policies.

At Runic, certain financial guarantees associated with sales of specialised products give rise to contingent losses which must be reported in a note to the company's balance sheet.[44] These contingencies have traditionally been reported by Runic on a basis that reveals the net potential liability after deducting the value of securities held against the guarantees offered. The securities take the form of assets which are specialised technological items and may be unique: external specialist valuers are employed, although the finance director described the valuation process as 'a bit of black magic'. This suggests that although, through conventional practice the valuer's technique and skills are effectively 'black boxed' (Callon and Latour, 1981), some doubt might exist about the numbers produced, particularly from the perspective of accounting objectivity. The valuation is itself a form of ceremonial which provides comfort[45]: although those involved in the process may well recognise its limitations in terms of 'objectivity', the process offers reassurance to the users of the company's published accounts. An alternative method of reporting contingent losses would be to report the gross potential liability, ignoring the value of the security.

A review of the Runic disclosure policy was prompted by two factors: decreasing asset values reported by the external valuers and an increasing level of contingent losses that were crystallising, due to customers encountering financial difficulties during a period of recession. Members of the audit committee had specific views on this issue, as Max Tinker reported: '..one factor that is influencing us here quite a lot is that we've got an American as a non exec and he is extremely conscious of the threat of being sued, whereas we go along in happy oblivion really ... and so he, for example, was all for gross disclosure because you can't fault it - once you've done it you certainly can't go back and you've given maximum disclosure, so he was all for that. We've got a banker and what do bankers want? They want to know what your exposure is, so he was for the gross as well..'

The minutes of the audit committee meeting held to discuss the draft accounts for 1994 gave a hint of the problem: In the area of sales financing, exposures were increasing due to the continued fall in [the second-hand value of the assets used as security] as advised by [the specialist valuers] and to the movement towards taking direct funding risk rather than the more traditional asset value guarantee risk. This required that the necessary level of funding was available and gave impetus to the need for a defined board policy and limits. [The company chairman] believed that this was a situation which had to be managed according to the strength of the [Runic] balance sheet' (Runic audit committee minutes, February 1994)

The final sentence from the minutes extract indicates that the company chairman was reluctant to move towards 'a defined board policy and limits' which would require more detailed disclosure. He wished to 'manage the situation' with regard to the expected level of crystallising losses in the context of the company's ability to meet these demands. He clearly saw little value in spelling out the detail of amounts which were unlikely to crystallise as losses: even hidden in the notes to the accounts, this could have the effect of weakening the balance sheet, sending signals to creditors and investors which might be interpreted adversely, affecting the company's share price and its ability to raise finance.

7.3   COMPETING NETWORKS: MOMENTS OF TRANSLATION

Here we see the beginning of the problematisation process. The audit committee members identified the problem[46] - the need for an accounting policy change - and raised the issue at the audit committee meeting. They were, however, faced with opposition to policy change from the company chairman, as observed from the minutes, and also from Max Tinker: '..we have disclosed the net exposure as a potential contingent liability for many years...The issue has now arisen as to whether we should show the gross exposure and I have argued that we should not, first of all because its a big number and will frighten people, secondly because it's a meaningless number because it assumes that the security has nil value and under no circumstances does it have nil value, we're only talking about what value it does have.'

Two networks can now be identified: the non executive directors comprising the audit committee, and the senior executive directors who already constitute a well established grouping, as Henry Morton explained:

'..the responsibilities are shared between these three [chairman, chief executive and finance director]- they are the dominant figures in the policy making and there wouldn't be any one person pushing the case, they'd be acting as a team collectively, there's never any apparent difference of opinion between those three so they've obviously talked it out themselves beforehand ..'

The impetus for policy change had, according to Max, been boosted by the particular concern of the American non executive director who was used to the more conservative approach of reporting the gross contingent loss figure required under US accounting rules. In explaining this, Max emphasised that there are no UK rules in this area: 'So that was a real case example where there's no ruling - if we had to do US GAAP[47] then we would have to disclose gross but under UK GAAP we don't and we're not listed in the United States.'

Thus neither the audit committee network nor the executive director network punctualised by Max Tinker was able to draw on any 'black box' in terms of ruling or precedent.

Although Max Tinker and his executive colleagues believed that the existing policy of net disclosure was appropriate, they recognised the increasing 'exposures' noted in the audit committee minutes and, in the context of plans to raise additional equity finance, were prepared to provide additional information. However, Max had argued strongly against gross disclosure, as noted in the extract quoted above, and so a compromise solution was proposed - net disclosure coupled with a sensitivity assessment. The current policy of net disclosure of the potential loss would thus be amplified by an indication of how this figure would change in relation to a change in the value of the security. Max Tinker explained this: '..we said 'OK, well here's our net figure - what would happen if the value of the security fell by x per cent?' Twenty per cent was the figure we chose and the potential exposure then becomes so and so and that was the way we put forward our accounts.'

Each network was aiming to persuade the full board of its views, a final process of enrolment and mobilisation which would result in the company's accounts being prepared on the basis of the 'winning' accounting policy. The first target for interessement and enrolment was the external audit team[48] headed by Ronald Roberts, who reported: '..at Runic this year for instance there was a specific issue that came up .. they [the audit committee] asked us for our specific advice on it - they said 'What is your specific advice on this particular issue?'

Although no detailed account of the discussions is available, Max Tinker's account indicates that the audit committee successfully enrolled the external auditor - but that this enrolment was only temporary: 'The auditors wanted us to show the gross value but they'd actually come off it and agreed with us that the net and the sensitivity was the way to do it... the auditors said 'We were in favour of the gross figure - it's very unusual to show sensitivity in accounts but we've been persuaded.'' (Max Tinker)

Ronald Roberts did not indicate what advice was given to the audit committee - it is not clear whether initial support from the auditors encouraged the members to persist in their proposal or whether the executive network had already enrolled the auditors before any advice was given to the audit committee. (The issue of the external auditor's relationships with the networks is discussed in more detail below.)

Having enrolled the external auditor, Max also acted to enrol and mobilise the 'unseen armies' of the users of Runic's accounts: '..the clinching argument was 'What is it that the shareholders and the bankers and so on are interested in?' They're interested in what happens if the value of the security falls and we're giving them a benchmark, not a graph that shows all the way, but we're giving them a pointer and that was the clinching argument - it certainly was for me.'

Ronald Roberts' comment indicates that the company's bankers were indeed consulted: '[The audit committee] considered it themselves and the board considered it and the bankers considered it and it was all to do with disclosure but they wanted to make sure that they really had everybody in the pot ....'

There is, however, no evidence that any attempt was made to determine shareholders' requirements in this regard - for example, by discussion with institutional shareholders. It is important to remember that all parties involved can claim to represent shareholder interests – all directors are elected by shareholders and the external auditors are employed to report to the shareholders.

The stronger network of the executive combined with the auditors then met again with the audit committee and formally presented the compromise proposal:
'..the circumstances[49] had highlighted the difficulties in predicting liabilities under asset value guarantees given to customers as part of a sales financing package. The continuing financial difficulties at ...[a customer] had led to a lot of discussion on the drafting of note...[the contingent loss note] A

revised note was tabled which included a broad sensitivity statistic based on a 20% reduction in second hand [asset] values. The alternative would be to give figures for the gross contingency as well as the net; this was regarded as potentially misleading because of the size of the figure which had to be seen in relation to the spread of risk. Recognising the disclosure requirements in connection with...[50], it was agreed that some further disclosure was prudent, although this did not go so far as to require the gross figures to be given.

[Ronald Roberts, the external auditor] confirmed that this conformed with current accounting standards. [A member of the audit committee] believed that giving the sensitivity example produced a spurious speculative contingent liability figure which could be arbitrarily misinterpreted. He believed it might be better to give the gross figure coupled with appropriate explanation.'(Runic audit committee minutes, March 1995)

As the last sentence indicates, the meeting was inconclusive: audit committee members would not agree to the tabled note and Max Tinker was asked to prepare a paper for the full board meeting setting out the pros and cons of each proposal, so that the issue could be fully debated.

Max Tinker's account indicates that the executive network almost fragmented at this point with some movement towards accepting the audit committee's view, perhaps because they believed that the remaining members of the main board would be enrolled by the non executive directors on the audit committee, and the argument would be lost in a public and potentially damaging way.

In any event, it would appear that the chairman needed to use all his influence to secure the desired outcome: 'In the audit committee it was left that we would take it away and think again which we did - our audit committee is approximately a week before the board meeting - so we went away and thought about it and we actually wavered and at one point in that week we were going to disclose the gross but by the time we came to the board meeting we were back on to the sensitivity so we had another debate at the board meeting and in fact it's ended up with sensitivity . But there's an issue - I mean, I can't say that all the directors agreed but in that sort of circumstance I'm afraid the chairman's facing a difficult task and I suppose he takes the majority.'(Max Tinker)

The board was finally enrolled by the executive network and the final accounts for 1995 carried a contingent loss note based on the net disclosure accompanied by a sensitivity assessment.

Consensus may be defined as the situation reached when participants are prepared to forsake their individual positions to enable the group to act with unanimity. It implies that participants have reached a level of comfort where further debate is not deemed necessary but it does not mean that all agree, only that all are at this point prepared to set aside their differences in order to move forward together. In ANT terms, consensus represents a conscious process of enrolment allowing the network to be mobilised.

7.4 THE NETWORK WEB: A NETWORK OF NETWORKS?

These stories may be read as an illustration of an audit committee acting in precisely the manner anticipated by Cadbury, demonstrating best practice in implementing high standards of corporate governance. The audit committee, an independent and forceful group, raised an issue of accountability and disclosure: its concern was to ensure that users of the company's accounts should have access to relevant and reliable information in an area where no clear legislative or regulatory guidance existed. Although the view of the audit committee was ultimately rejected by the main board, the issues were openly debated. The network represented by the finance director comprised the chairman and the chief executive and the external auditor: these allies were enrolled on the basis of the finance director's argument that the audit committee approach was unnecessarily conservative and could indeed be damaging - could 'frighten people' - and the claim of this network to represent the best interests of the users of the company's accounts.

No attempt was apparently made to influence the audit committee other than in formal debate. Henry Morton did not discuss this specific example but contrasted his experience at Runic with his experience of chairing an audit committee elsewhere: '..whereas in another company I know where there's a very very aggressive - very pleasant but very aggressive - chairman who has very determined ideas, he would, if he had a contentious issue, have raised it with me several times before it ever got near the audit committee by telephoning me, meeting me to do whatever, so each has its own style - it depends upon the people.'

However, the stories are incomplete. Henry Morton, although happy to give more detailed information about incidents relating to his equivalent position in other companies in the past, would not be drawn on any specific issue relating to Runic. The accounts given by Max Tinker and Ronald Roberts, together with careful reading of the audit committee minutes, seem to indicate that he adopted a neutral position during the events described.

Perhaps more crucially, we also have no information about the processes through which the external auditor was influenced to change from one network to the other: an important influence here may have been another network, less distinct than those already outlined, linking the finance director, the audit committee chair and the external auditor and revealed in the interviews with Ronald Roberts and with Henry Morton.

Henry Morton had also chaired the audit committee of another company, Tiffin, for many years. The auditors of Tiffin had more recently won the tender for the audit of Runic and Henry had a close working relationship with the audit team - the same team for both companies. In discussing channels of communication between audit committee participants, he observed that communication was facilitated by these established relationships: 'I meet XYZ socially anyway and from time to time at other meetings and other occasions.. when we meet we have chats and they would quite often ring me up about something.'

Ronald Roberts confirmed that these equivalent roles at Tiffin brought him into contact with Henry Morton more frequently than might be the normal case. He also revealed a friendly relationship with Max Tinker who had first joined Runic (at a lower level) at the same time as Ronald became involved in the audit team: '..we sort of grew up in that respect together so I got to know him very well...we know each other sort of from a business and a personal sense.'

It would appear that such relationships are not unusual: Hussey and Jack (1995), in a study of the relationship between the finance director and the auditor, reported that the most important characteristic influencing the appointment of external auditors is the personal chemistry between the finance director and the local audit partner (See also Beattie et al, 2001). The consequent challenge to auditor independence is discussed in more detail in chapter 8. Although participants are quick to assert that such close relationships are essential to the effective performance of their duties and are bounded by unwritten codes of 'professionalism', it is not difficult to envisage a situation in which the existence of such informal relationships might be used as interessement/enrolment devices serving to undermine what appear superficially to be sound corporate governance mechanisms. An alternative reading of the Runic stories brings this less distinct network into the foreground to examine its influence, with a particular focus on the role of the external auditor.

7.5   THE NETWORK ASSOCIATIONS OF THE EXTERNAL AUDITOR

The extensive literature on the 'expectation gap' (see, for example, Humphrey, 1997) underlines the ambiguity perceived in the role of the external auditor. The auditor's report certifying that the company's accounts present a 'true and fair view' is addressed to the members of the company (the shareholders) although the auditor has no direct contact with this group. Formally appointed by the shareholders at the annual general meeting, the auditor is effectively employed by the company and, in order to undertake the duties of the audit role, must work closely with company management. The possibility of adverse influence by management, against the interests of the shareholders, is a fundamental assumption of the agency model and is widely recognised in the literature on auditor independence, although an alternative view has been suggested by Wolnizer (1995) and by Grout et al (1994) , discussed in chapter 8.

The Cadbury Code reflects the view that auditor independence is fundamental to sound corporate governance and recommends the audit committee as a safeguard for this independence, enabling the non executive directors and the external auditor to join together to support the interests of shareholders in the face of pressure from the company executive. Section 5 (Cadbury Committee, 1992) sets out the Committee's approach in detail:

'The central issue is to ensure that an appropriate relationship exists between the auditors and the management whose financial statements they are auditing. Shareholders require auditors to work with and not against management, while always remaining professionally objective...An essential first step must be the development of more effective accounting standards. Accounting standards provide important reference points against which auditors exercise their professional judgement. Their position is strengthened if standards do not allow alternative accounting treatments.... A second step should be the formation by every listed company of an audit committee which gives the auditors direct access to the non-executive members of the board. Shareholders look to the audit committee to ensure that the relationship between the auditors and management remains objective and that the auditors are able to put their views in the event of any difference of opinion with management.' (Cadbury Committee, 1992:38)

From an ANT perspective, this identifies the external auditor as a punctualised actor representing the shareholders and using the audit committee and the 'black boxed' resources of the Cadbury Code and accounting standards to enrol executive management.

In the context of these general assumptions about the role of the external auditor, let us consider the situation as revealed at Runic. The contingent loss situation outlined above is very specific to Runic and its particular customers and markets. The accounting standard covering this area, SSAP 18, requires disclosure but permits a wide range of possible approaches, precisely because of the recognition that companies are likely to differ widely in their specific situation and that generalised rules may lead to inappropriate reporting (an argument against accounting standards developed by Baxter, 1981). In this case, therefore, the external auditor was required to exercise professional judgement without the support of clearly stated guidance.

From the Cadbury perspective, we might expect the external auditor to support the audit committee approach - the demand for the more conservative gross disclosure - and, indeed, it is clear from Max Tinker's account that this was the first position: 'The auditors wanted us to show the gross value but they'd actually come off it and agreed with us that the net and the sensitivity was the way to do it. the auditors said 'We were in favour of the gross figure - it's very unusual to show sensitivity in accounts but we've been persuaded'.

Max suggests that the change in the external auditor's view was effected through an appeal to user requirements: '..the clinching argument was 'What is it that the shareholders and the bankers and so on are interested in?' They're interested in what happens if the value of the security falls and we're giving them a benchmark, not a graph that shows all the way, but we're giving them a pointer and that was the clinching argument - it certainly was for me.' - but Ronald Roberts made no comment on the switch. However, his general comments on the pattern of relationships surrounding the audit committee are more illuminating:

'.. one says 'Well, what is the role of the auditor in relation to the audit committee and the finance director and should the finance director actually let the auditors in a sense help him steer things through at audit committees or should the audit committee look to the auditors as a direct link to them?' and I think my own view is that its both - the finance director looks to us to do certain things to help him... Well, sometimes we actually in a sense impose our advice through Max to the audit committee on specific issues ...there are issues within Runic where we say to Max: 'We suggest that you say this that and the other' and so we would draft things for him..... We'd say to Max: 'We are going to do this, we are going to produce papers on this, that and the other because we feel it's right for the audit committee' and we would hope that he would see that as a positive move rather than trying to take things away from him - you know things like 'What are the key issues in the group?' - we would issue a highlights memorandum for the audit committee - that is, then going straight to the audit committee to do with it, as it were, what they want and we would debate that with them fully ... we like to have as much as possible fairly open debate with the audit committee there and we indeed we do say, at the end of the audit committee meeting there, we ask the executive directors to leave and then they can discuss whatever they want to discuss with us ...'

This account offers three models of relationships between the finance director, the audit committee and the external auditor.

The first - '.. the finance director looks to us to do certain things to help him' - implies enrolment of the external auditor by the executive network, a situation apparently fraught with potential threat to shareholder interests through the compromise of auditor independence. However, in areas where standard accounting practice has yet to be developed, or requires rethinking due to changes in the business environment, innovation or improvement is unlikely without the initiative being taken by the preparers of accounting statements, with whom the responsibility and accountability ultimately rests.

This point was expressed by Alex Anderson at Glengarry: '.. the point to make really is that we are responsible for our accounts, the auditors are there to audit them, and it's a much harder challenge for us to be comfortable that we're doing things the right way than it is to convince the auditors that we're doing it right ...I think that's a very important point to make and one that I do make to the directors, you know, it's not a matter of convincing the auditors to accept some sort of sporty treatment but actually are we comfortable that it is the right treatment?'

From this perspective, enrolment of the external auditors is a positive advantage, when it has been achieved through rational argument and the exercise of professional judgement (see also Grout et al, 1994, discussed in chapter 8)

The second model has the problematisation undertaken by the external auditor who then seeks to enrol the audit committee, either by initially enrolling the finance director: '..sometimes we actually in a sense impose our advice through [Max Tinker] to the audit committee on specific issues..' or by a more direct approach: '..We'd say to [Max Tinker] 'We are going to do this, we are going to produce papers on this that and the other because we feel it's right for the audit committee' and we would hope that he would see that as a positive move rather than trying to take things away from him - you know things like 'What are the key issues in the group?' - we would issue a highlights memorandum for the audit committee - that is, then going straight to the audit committee to do with it, as it were, what theywant..'

The third model implies problematisation by the audit committee, followed by enrolment of the external auditor: '..we do say, at the end of the audit committee meeting there, we ask the executive directors to leave and then they can discuss whatever they want to discuss with us..'

From a Cadbury perspective, the third model would presumably fit the expectations of how an audit committee should operate, with the second model also acceptable. The first model would be more questionable: in assessing this, much would depend on the process of interessement - if the enrolment of the auditor was based on a process of rational argument this might be acceptable, whereas undue pressure (threat of auditor change, for example) would not. Within these two extremes lies a variety of possible interessement devices. A process of interessement and enrolment which did not compromise the independence of the parties involved would have greater acceptability: the perception of independence would underpin and validate the consensus achieved. This point is discussed in more detail in chapter 8.

The events at Runic appear to begin with the last model but shift rapidly to the first. The process of interessement and enrolment is not transparent from the accounts available but has been presented as one of rational argument. However, the existence of the other network identified must be influential here, acting as an interessement device itself. Again we may discern a range of perspectives within two extremes. From one view, the second network could be seen as a mechanism to 'smooth the path', ensuring swift and amicable communication between the parties involved: from another, it could be viewed as a means of exerting more subtle pressure, encouraging dissenting members to set aside differences in order to maintain the network, and thus to conform.

ANT analysis of the Runic stories has thus demonstrated the formation and re-formation of networks involved in resolving a specific issue. Examination of the processes of interessement and enrolment underscores the fragility of these networks. The core 'executive' and 'audit committee' networks remained stable during the period covered by these events but the enrolment of the external auditor in each network consecutively demonstrated the speed and impact of change that is possible and emphasised the need to consider the role and nature of interessement devices, which may well include membership of other networks.

7.6 CONSENSUS: AN ENROLMENT DEVICE AND A COMMODITY

At Runic, the finance director, the audit committee chair and the external auditor all emphasised that both formal and informal communication were vital in ensuring that the work of the audit committee could proceed in a helpful fashion, and saw their informal relationships as a great strength. The suggestion that these relationships might damage auditor independence from the Cadbury perspective was strongly countered by the arguments that independence was secured through the appropriately 'objective' behaviour of professional people, that the existence of mechanisms such as the audit committee could not prevent individuals determined to commit wrongdoing and that it would be impossible to operate effectively in any other way. Similar views were expressed by other participants.

Bailey (1965) noted the importance of such relationships:

'..they [committee members] must be wary of trampling too heavily on one another's corns, because they require favours of one another in other spheres and other committees; a mode of social interaction which the perceptive Cornford [Cornford, 1953] calls 'squaring'. It is to be noted that a consensual decision reached through squaring is only possible when a small number of people are concerned, and when they interact with one another in several different situations. We are not saying that this frequency of interaction enforces a consensual decision: only that the 'horse-trading' negotiations which can lead to consensus are only possible when there is a frequency of interaction.'(1965:11)

The account of events at Runic further demonstrates the paradox of the audit committee: at one level, the stories illustrate an audit committee operating in precisely the way envisaged by Cadbury, but an exploration of the networks surrounding the audit committee reveals that it is the existence of such networks, and the negotiations that underpin shifting enrolment between them, that enable the committee to perform in this apparently 'effective' manner. The existence of these networks directly contradicts the Cadbury emphasis on independence, undermining the concept through the establishment of close working relationships. Meyer and Rowan's notion of decoupling is again observed here. (see section 5.6)

My own initial problematisation centred on an exploration of areas of contention. Through shifting the focus of problematisation to consensus achievement rather than conflict resolution, interviewees asserted that consensus was achieved by negotiation through networks of relationships that did not harm shareholders' or lenders interests and indeed demonstrated a high level of concern for them, although theoretically such relationships undermined independence and 'infringed' the prescriptions for good corporate governance.

This suggests that, for valid demonstration of consensus, such consensus must be seen to be arrived at in a way that does not compromise the independence of those involved – indeed, there is a need to perform the achievement of consensus in a way which emphasises such independence, through rational debate. Yet the practical achievement of consensus is effected paradoxically through networks which appear to undermine the notion of independence because they are based on close relationships between participants.

The achievement of consensus is itself an interessement/enrolment device since it confers individual benefits – participants are seen as reasonable people who are prepared to compromise for the common good and act as part of an effective team.

The re-problematisation may also be interpreted as a device to enrol me in confirming the self-presentation of the individuals concerned[51].

Consensus assists ceremonial in the achievement of its purpose, as Myerhoff (1977:222) observed: ' ..all rituals are dramas of persuasion. They are didactic, enacted pronouncements concerning the meaning of an occasion, and the nature and worth of the people involved in the occasion. In many ways rituals may be judged like any drama – they must be convincing. Not all the parties involved need to be equally convinced or equally moved. But the whole of it must be good enough to play...the appearance of attention is essential, and everyone is in it together...all must collude so as not to spoil the show...'

Consensus serves an important purpose at an organisational level. The desire to establish consensus can be explained in terms of comfort: for example, Power (1997:126) noted that adversarial reporting produces discomfort and there are significant pressures to constrain the level of criticism in audit reports to an acceptable indication that the audit is 'adding value' in assisting management through its critique. The ultimate critical expression of the qualified audit report is rare.[52]

Consensus of the audit committee reported to the main board offers comfort and reassurance that specific issues relating to monitoring and control have been comprehensively dealt with by a small group of 'experts' – 'black boxed' in ANT terms (Callon and Latour, 1981). Black boxes provide comfort and reassurance: a neat and tidy parcel of assumptions that may be taken for granted and do not need to be unpacked. However, the value of this consensus appears to be intimately linked with independence – consensus achieved through 'undue influence' would have less value than that achieved through a visible process. As Alex Anderson emphasised: '..meetings which are strictly scripted are actually pretty unproductive. We can all read out the papers and everyone nods and says 'Yes, agreed' ...[a productive meeting is] where you've got real issues where you clearly present the facts, you know, if someone has a question they're prepared to ask it, or a different point of view is stated.'

Such meetings are unproductive in that they do not produce a consensus validated by demonstrations of independence. Consensus may thus be viewed as a commodity produced within the audit committee with a worth or value which is dependent on the process through which it is seen to be generated. Crucial within this process is the demonstration of independence, discussed in the next chapter.

Chapter 8:
INDEPENDENCE

In chapter 7 it was suggested that consensus is a commodity produced by the audit committee with a value which determines the level of comfort such consensus may generate for the main board, and that this value is derived from demonstrations of independence among those arriving at consensus. In this chapter, assumptions about the relationship between financial reporting quality and the independence of external auditors are discussed in relation to the role of the audit committee. Participants' stories which illustrate their understandings of independence are recounted. The performance of independence within the audit committee through questioning is examined and the use of independence as a commodity and interessement device is explored.

8.1   THE IMPORTANCE OF INDEPENDENCE: THE CADBURY PERSPECTIVE

The manifestation of independence is of considerable importance within the corporate environment. Relationships between companies are under constant scrutiny in order to identify dependencies permitting potential concentrations of power which may distort or constrain markets. Given the complexity of industry and group structures and the multiplicity of transactional relationships, the notion of 'total independence' within such relationships is a goal of unlikely attainment: there is, however, a need to acknowledge the existence of, and risks inherent in, situations where unequal relationships may lead to economic consequences perceived as adverse. Disclosure of the existence of such relationships allows those who may be affected to assess the risks involved. For example, the accounting consequences of transactions undertaken within subsidiary, associate, joint venture and related party relationships are reported in accordance with a series of Statements of Standard Accounting Practice (SSAPs) and Financial Reporting Standards (FRSs).

The corporate governance literature surveyed in chapter 2 suggests that the traditional stewardship approach of accountability through disclosure is inadequate in the context of modern expectations of corporate governance: among the suggestions for improvement is the strengthening of the exercise of independent judgement by external auditors and non executive directors (NEDs). A number of studies and reports have explored the problem of requiring NEDs to act as monitors as well as advisors (e.g. Binder Hamlyn,1994; Ezzamel and Watson, 1997; PricewaterhouseCoopers, 2001). It is not clear that all NEDs perceive this as a problem: Bob Cunningham, for example, a widely experienced NED, explained that the role of the NED was not to perform a direct monitoring function but to ensure that systems were in place that required the executive directors to monitor themselves (he did not offer any explicit examples of how this would work in practice). The literature on auditor independence and NED independence addresses definitions of independence, threats to it and possible solutions to such threats but does not consider the broader role played by independence expounded in this chapter.

Agreed outcomes in the context of a relationship with clearly unbalanced dependencies are presumed to be more easily achieved because of the exercise of the power resulting from the dominance of one party or coalition of parties. Such a consensus is generally viewed as having less value than a similar outcome among a group of independent individuals who arrive at consensus through the exercise of objective judgement and rationality, unclouded by subjective influence. The ANT analysis in chapter 7 effectively demonstrates that 'formally' independent relationships - those generating high value consensus - may in fact be subtly altered within the surrounding network of other networks where complex alliances, temporary and fragile though they may be, affect outcomes.

The audit committee offers an arena for the demonstration of independence. Its existence requires (to comply with the Cadbury Code) the appointment to the board of directors of a minimum of three individuals who are expected to demonstrate their personal independence, thus guaranteeing the independence of the external auditor, enhancing the credibility of the company's financial statements and ultimately the standing of the company in the eyes of finance providers. The audit committee 'produces' consensus which reassures the main board, and hence the users of company reports, that the specific issues within the remit of the audit committee have been appropriately dealt with. This consensus is validated by the degree of independence associated with those who arrive at it. Thus the audit committee also 'produces' independence.

Through all participants' accounts of audit committee activity, a common thread of reference to 'independence' could be discerned. All respondents described 'independence' (or associated ideas of 'objectivity' and 'personal integrity') as a characteristic of audit committee members which was fundamental to their understanding of audit committee effectiveness. ' Independence from management' was specifically identified as a factor which might contribute to audit committee effectiveness in Collier (1992) and was thus included in the questionnaire for ranking by respondents. Most respondents also included a further emphasis on independence in their answers to the open questions.

The importance accorded to the concept of independence would thus appear to match the Cadbury perspective outlined in figure 1: this assumes a link between the independence of auditors, underpinned by the independence of the non-executive directors forming the audit committee, and an improved quality of financial reporting which in turn supports the development of higher standards of corporate governance.

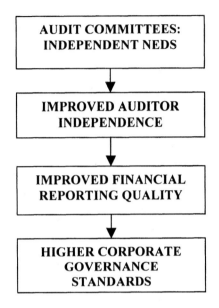

Figure 1: The Cadbury Perspective

The Cadbury recommendations focus on the independence of non-executive directors who, by virtue of their status, have 'independence from executive responsibility' (Cadbury Committee, 1992:20) and are expected to 'bring an independent judgement to bear on issues of strategy, performance, resources...and standards of conduct.' (1992:22) They should 'be independent of management and free from any business or other relationship which could materially interfere with the exercise of their independent judgement' (1992:22) and the probity of their relationship with the board should be demonstrated by 'a formal selection process, which will reinforce the independence of non-executive director..'(1992:23) Length of tenure may compromise this independent status: 'Non-executive directors may lose something of their independent edge, if they remain on a board too long.'(1992:23) The underlying assumption is that the independence of non-executive directors will afford an increased level of auditor independence, through the operation of the audit committee.

As Power (1997:132) observed: 'There is a deeply held view that without independence, audit has no value.' However, although problematic outcomes may be ascribed to lack of auditor independence, the existence of apparent threats to independence does not inevitably lead to the undermining of accountability processes. Gwilliam (1987) commented: 'Independence is ultimately a psychological construct and the appearance of non-independence is only indicative of the likelihood of non-independent behaviour.' (1987:105)

Wolnizer's critique of audit independence (Wolnizer,1987) was based on the argument that the conventional accounting notion of independence is incomplete since it is based only on the mental attributes of the individual auditor and the relationships between auditors and their clients. He asserted that: '..the presumption that any steps taken to strengthen the independent status of auditors will lead of themselves to more 'objective' financial statements is unfounded.'(1995:54) - because independence of evidence - the capability of external verification of the content of accounting statements - is the key to objective financial reporting. Drawing parallels with medicine and law where practitioners base judgements on independently verifiable evidence, he concluded that: 'Unless accounting practices are reformed so that financial statements can be authenticated by recourse to reliable commercial evidence, audit committees are red herrings' (Wolnizer, 1995:45)

Power (1997) developed Wolnizer's argument by demonstrating that the character of independently verifiable evidence is not an intrinsic quality but depends on socially negotiated agreement. Power's notion of epistemic independence captures the essence of this problem: 'Where clear rules of auditee conduct and robust techniques for determining compliance with those rules exist, the audit process is epistemically independent of the auditee. The auditor may be dependent on some information from the auditee but the basis on which conclusions are drawn is independent.' (1997:133)

Where epistemic independence is limited, rules are indeterminate or ambiguous and auditor and auditee must necessarily negotiate to establish the existence of compliance or breach.

Ezzamel and Watson (1997) also cast doubt on the ability of audit committees to fulfil the Cadbury expectations, with regard to guaranteeing auditor independence, observing that Cadbury did not provide sufficient detail about the purpose of the audit committee or how such purpose is to be achieved in practice, as noted in section 2.2.1.

Beattie et al (1997) provided evidence that audit partners and finance directors view audit committees as a major factor in enhancing auditor independence but they offered no indication of *why* respondents believed audit committees to be so important or *how* audit committees achieved this enhancement.

The next link in the chain - the presumption that improved auditor independence leads to improved financial reporting - has also been challenged by Grout et al (1994) who demonstrated that remedies introduced to deter practices seen as compromising independence did not necessarily have the desired effect: they suggested that a degree of auditor dependence on clients may in fact improve the quality of financial reports. Power (1997:29) described the relationship between the costs of audit and the assurance levels provided as obscure and noted that: '..it is not obvious that making financial auditors more independent, whatever that means, will maintain or enhance the existing cost-assurance relation.'

8.2 CONCEPTIONS OF INDEPENDENCE

Within the literature on auditor independence, a distinction is frequently made between independence in fact and independence in appearance (see, for example, Wallman, 1996; Falk and Frucot, 1997). Bartlett (1993) quoted definitions of independence in fact and independence in appearance taken from US auditing standards. The former relates to the mental attitude of the auditor and is difficult to establish in an 'objective' fashion. The latter relates to circumstances which could be perceived as threatening independence and which may be controlled, in order to demonstrate the necessary distancing which is seen as fundamental to objectivity. 'To *be* independent, the auditor must be intellectually honest; to be recognized as independent, he must be free from any obligation to or interest in the client, its management, or its owners.' (AICPA, 1991, quoted in Bartlett, 1993:55). In the UK, the ICAEW Guide to Professional Ethics does not make this distinction explicit but initially stresses the fundamental role of individual integrity before describing a series of potential threats to auditor independence and offering guidance on their practical avoidance or minimisation (ICAEW, 1997b). The limited literature addressing the issue of audit committee independence does not dwell on this distinction.

However, it would appear that, among participants in this study, a similar distinction is generally accepted with regard to the independence of audit committee members. Two aspects of independence were identified in participants' stories. The first relates to a personal quality found in a particular individual, defined here as *independence of mind* (equivalent to independence in fact) and the second represents a notion of distance and detachment which is assumed to be essential to objective judgement, defined here as *independence of connection* (equivalent to independence in appearance)[53].

A link between the two aspects may be discerned in situations where close relationships exist which may be interpreted as compromising independence of connection. At Glengarry, Martin Johnson, the audit committee chair, had previously been the company finance director; at Runic, complex interrelationships had developed between audit committee participants through roles in other companies (described in chapter 7) and Henry Morton, the audit committee chair, had served in this capacity for almost ten years. In every interview with these participants, the close relationships or length of service were cited as important to audit committee operations, helping those involved to do a better job through close familiarity with the company concerned: in every case it was argued that the objectivity of judgement to be derived from independence of connection was not compromised through these relationships but was guaranteed by 'professionalism', by the personal qualities of the individuals involved. This individual quality - independence of mind - is seen to provide even greater assurance of independent and objective judgement than the concept of independence of connection, which can be more clearly defined and monitored.

As Samet and Sherman (1984:55) observed: 'The effectiveness of the audit committee will depend more upon it being composed of dedicated individuals with a deep sense of personal commitment to the company and its shareholders, than being composed of individuals formally independent of management.'

Varying approaches to the demonstration of independence of mind could be observed in the self-presentation of individuals during discussions on this topic. Martin Johnson presented himself as 'hero'. He described his career prior to his appointment at Glengarry in great detail[54], emphasising that he had always been in favour of audit committees and had established one at every company where he had been employed as finance director, long before they became common: 'I've been doing this a long time, I've been chief financial officer of public companies since I was 31, that's a long time. I've always been a finance director who likes to have a proper structure in place - I formed an audit committee at [ABC plc] when I became the first finance director there that they'd ever had ..'

However, it was almost impossible to get him to answer direct questions about how these audit committees actually worked. His overall demeanour was that of someone used to being interviewed by journalists, deflecting questions on areas that he did not wish to explored. When questioned about the apparent threat to his independent status as a non executive director of Glengarry from his previous relationship with the company as its finance director, he presented a curious answer: 'It's sometimes forgotten that the finance director of a big sprawling multinational group himself is actually the most independent person - he's not actually in operations at all, he is effectively the chairman and chief executive's right hand to make sure you keep everybody honest.'

This seemed to imply that there was no difference between his role as finance director and as non executive director, an unusual perspective on both roles. The implication of Martin's relationship with the company is explored in more detail in section 8.3.

Alex Anderson's relationship with Glengarry was equally complex. He had previously acted as the engagement partner on the company's audit. He gave a practised account of the advantages to Glengarry of such a situation (quoted in section 8.3), giving the impression that the issue had been raised many times before, and insisting that the independence of the external auditors was not affected in any way. He presented himself as objective, fair-minded, not influenced by previous working relationships: '.. it certainly doesn't cause problems in terms of conflict. I have absolutely no doubt where my responsibilities lie.'

Henry Morton's self-presentation relied on an amusing and self-deprecating approach. He commented on our shared professional training and used this to help me to identify with his position (noted in section 3.3). Although Henry is an individual of considerable standing within the business community, his manner did not reflect this status. Describing the seating arrangements for the Runic audit committee, he commented: '..I just edge along and go into the chairman's seat very tentatively..'

Referring to the chairman of another company where he had been a non executive director, he observed: '..I think he drew some comfort from the fact that he had some fairly important non executive directors around him - not including me, I was one of the less important... plenty of double barrelled names with lots of ministerial and other experience..'

He laughed a lot during the interview, and his comments were often humorous in style: '..you know, if I were still a finance director I'd jolly well have to alter my ways!'

Henry's relationship with the previous Runic chairman had been close: they had filled the same roles at Tiffin plc, working with the same audit team – again, a relationship which could be perceived as a threat to independence. Henry's approach was to acknowledge this: '..he [previous Runic chairman] used to chair it [the audit committee], which was, I suppose, a little bit naughty but I knew [him] quite well and I think when he brought me in he started the audit committee and although he chaired it I think he did look to me to advise him, we were very close so I think it worked alright but of course with the chairman of the company also being chairman of the audit committee some things could be steam-rollered through if one has to honest about it..'

Combined with his charming manner, this straightforward recognition of possible imperfections was designed to be disarming and to reassure as to his independence.

All three individuals were concerned to present themselves as independent in mind, although in each case their independence of connection might be called into question.

8.3   THREATS TO AUDIT COMMITTEE INDEPENDENCE

The Cadbury Code envisaged threats to audit committee members independence arising from financial relationships (section 4.12 recommends that NEDs should have no other business relationship with the company; section 4.13 recommends that while fees should be adequate to reflect the time spent on the company's affairs, share option scheme participation and pensions are inappropriate), from 'patronage' (section 4.15 recommends a 'formal selection process' for NED appointments) and from length of tenure (section 4.16). Additionally, the Committee recognised a need for a sufficiently weighty NED presence on the board, section 4.11 recommending the appointment of a minimum of three NEDs.

However, finance directors and internal auditors interviewed indicated that the most problematic limitation to the useful contribution of NEDs was not lack of independence but lack of understanding of the company. These accounts expressed tones of disappointment rather than satisfaction that such NEDs would be easy to manipulate, as these examples indicate:

'I'm not sure I've yet got them quite to understand the range of work we cover, the sorts of things we come up with and how its progressed in the business .. they're almost taking a simplistic view…it's a little more shaded and complicated than I think perhaps they think at the moment….having said that, the quality of non-execs is probably improving ..[newly appointed NED] is probably the most heavy hitting business man that we've had…[he] could be valuable – I could imagine him saying 'In my company...this is a hot issue at the moment' and if that general steer came, that would be quite good.. [the other NEDs] bring their perspectives to things but not quite the understanding of the business of running a business…most of the others are halfway to the golf course, if not already on it' (Robin Dunston, Scrimshaw)
'..it's so easy in maturity when you're a non exec to start pontificating but when you're the finance director of a company, it tends to become yours - now yours in the nicest sense, you know, that you're just protecting it and you're doing what you think is right and these other fellows around, these non execs, are quite useless really, they don't really understand the issues..' (Henry Morton, Runic)

These comments may be intended to demonstrate the inevitability of management influence over NEDs, in the face of their lack of experience of the company (or even lack of interest in developing such experience, as Robin Dunston's last comment suggests). Participants indicated that independence of connection may undermine the potential contribution of NEDs, although this may be overcome as familiarity with the company develops over time – a further argument against the independence of connection supposedly derived from limited tenure. Several participants observed that it will take considerable time for a non-executive director to be able to contribute effectively in a complex company: 'I have an advantage in having been a non exec here for quite a long time - now I believe the pensions body [PIRC] at the moment are saying you become an insider if you're here for more than ten years - I think I've been here for about ten years. I see their point but also a company like [Runic] doesn't half take a long time to understand what's going on.' (Henry Morton)

This suggests that generalised rules about length of tenure may be inappropriate.

The effect of length of tenure on independence has been examined with varying conclusions. Ecton and Reinstein (1982) reported that new committee members ask the 'best' (a quality not defined) questions and suggested on this basis that rotation of membership would achieve greater audit committee effectiveness. However, Spangler and Braiotta (1990) assumed that a transactional leadership style underpinned effectiveness and suggested that membership continuity achieved by long tenure was necessary to develop this.

More subtle threats to audit committee independence may arise from other close relationships: significant relationships may exist between finance directors and external auditors which impact on audit committee operations. At Glengarry and Harrier, the finance directors were the companies' former external audit partners; Alex Anderson, the Glengarry finance director, described the advantages of having been a partner at PQ, Glengarry's auditors:

'.. well I'm gamekeeper turned poacher I suppose…quite a number of people have left [PQ] at partner level and moved to clients…it certainly doesn't cause problems in terms of conflict. I have absolutely no doubt where my responsibilities lie. It does have huge advantages in that I understand exactly how [PQ] works and therefore when we're looking to get the best people to do the work, when we're considering who should do particular assignments, particular special work, you know, we know who to go to and we know the areas on the other side where [PQ] are not particularly strong …so I'm very well placed to maximise value for shareholders out of that relationship and do that in a very productive and business like way.. relationships have worked very well here, I mean I knew people well before I joined - it was a great advantage joining a client rather than joining a company that I didn't know that much about, you know, I'd been to many of the key locations, I understood the business, you know, I'm almost a natural fit for this sort of position.…from the client's point of view again it's a lower risk appointment than going for someone who may have shone in interviews and assessments but you really don't know that much about..'

These appear to be well rehearsed arguments. Hussey and Jack (1995) indicated that this situation is not uncommon[55], and that 'personal chemistry' between the finance director and audit partner is a major factor in auditor appointments (see also Beattie et al, 2001). There is a fine balance to be struck between the professional friendships that make a good working relationship possible and the personal friendships which may be perceived as compromising independence. It is difficult to see how the audit committee can, in practice, influence the impact of such relationships: as an obligatory passage point, it may become ineffective when such networks strengthen.

At Glengarry, Martin Johnson, the audit committee chair was the former finance director: he acknowledged that there had been some criticism by PIRC about his status as an independent director but argued that his situation was unique in that he 'was involved in that difficult period and was involved in setting up the control culture' so his experience of the company was of particular value. (see section 5.5) Martin dismissed PIRC's criticism of his anomalous position with the observations that the other non executive directors were 'very independent' and 'They know I'm a very independent person'. Independence as a personality trait was here used to indicate 'I am prepared to make a nuisance of myself ': indeed, Simon Middleton, the internal auditor, described him causing considerable tension at audit committee meetings by 'worrying at issues like a dog with a bone'. His relationship with company management clearly remained close but the effect of this closeness seemed to be that he was continuing to act as an executive influence, rather than being influenced by management. His involvement in such areas appeared to be welcome – Alex Anderson commented: 'We have operations in a number of countries with soft currencies, you know, just thinking through how we manage our exposures in those countries - I mean, so there's actually been quite a lot of correspondence with him either on the phone or in writing on exactly what we ought to do in those areas, so that's an example of where we've had the benefit of his input outside the formal audit committee.'

However, Simon Middleton, expressed the view that this blurring of role contributed to what he described as the 'rather tense relationship' between the audit committee chair and the company chairman which was played out in audit committee meetings.

Such influence may potentially draw the audit committee into areas beyond the standard Cadbury terms of reference: indeed, Martin Johnson explained that he saw the audit committee role developing into strategic direction, once internal control procedures had become well established and merely required monitoring[56]. Other participants saw this as inappropriate:

'One of the problems there has been with [Runic] is that they are so keen to do the right thing that you could easily find yourself in the situation that you weren't non-executive, that you were executive - where one's been invited into some discussions.... you can lose your objectivity and you become involved with the decision and what you should be doing is not taking the decision but vetting the decision. It's difficult ground this - one which an accommodating management, wishing to do the right thing, occasionally can go too far in one way I think.' (Henry Morton)

There is also evidence that external auditors may exert more influence over their clients than is assumed in the Cadbury model. Eichenseher & Shields (1985) demonstrated the influence of major accountancy firms in encouraging clients to establish audit committees, observing that audit firms have considerable incentives to do so, since, for no cost to the firm, they enhance auditor independence and may well protect from allegations of fraud. Further evidence of the keen interest of external auditors in the operation of audit committees is the extensive production of advice in this area for clients by large accountancy firms and professional accountancy bodies, as noted in the literature review in chapter 2. Audit partner Ken Palmer admitted: 'We have a vested interest in making sure audit committees work the way we want'.

From an ANT perspective, threats to audit committee member independence, such as financial and business relationships and length of tenure, are interessement devices, deployed in attempts to enrol members in networks such as those linking finance directors with external auditors. In theory the audit committee acts as an obligatory passage point but in practice networks such as those identified in chapter 7 act to circumvent this. Networks form and re-form in relation to specific issues. Independence of connection becomes less relevant as time passes and the audit committee member creates essential working relationships: the NED's most important 'defence' against enrolment is independence of mind. If independence of mind can be demonstrated, there will be greater confidence among observers that, when enrolment in these networks is inevitable, objectivity will be maintained. One way of demonstrating independence of mind within the ceremonial activity of the audit committee meeting is by asking questions.

8.4   PERFORMANCE OF INDEPENDENCE: THE ASKING OF QUESTIONS

A factor of prime importance in participants' accounts in relation to independence of NEDs was the asking of questions. Questioning appears to be an important feature of audit committee work: audit committee members are expected to ask questions (for example, see Ecton and Reinstein,1982; Sommer 1991), although Tricker (1978:61) quotes a US commentator who observed that the role of the audit committee was very limited: 'Although questions are asked, not much can be done about the answers.'

Skill in questioning is seen as a prime quality in an effective NED. The US practitioner journal <u>Directors & Boards</u> carries short articles about individuals who are considered outstanding by their peers: Alden (1996) wrote about Philip Caldwell who was credited with a major impact at Digital Equipment Corporation: 'The pressure he exerted through discerning questions asked as chairman of the audit committee and in private sessions with management contributed much to the pace and success of the recovery...He was firm but polite in his incisive questions to management and our independent auditors. He was patient but would not tolerate easy answers. But at the same time he did not dominate board or committee discussions.'(1996:77)

Spencer (1983:40) quoted an interviewee: 'The central role of the non-executive director is the asking of awkward questions. His other role is getting the answers. For this, a high order of skill is needed, both social and technical.'

Three iterative levels of questioning may be identified. The first focuses on questions that are anticipated and to which answers may have already been supplied to the questioner, often in the form of written documentation. The asking and answering of such questions is a form of procedural ceremony which may be used to establish the relative positions of the questioner and questionee and the context of subsequent questions. At the second level questions have also been anticipated but answers, although readily accessible, have not been pre-produced. At the third level questions are potentially more challenging – they have not been anticipated and the provision of satisfactory answers requires careful thought and possibly further research.   From the perspective of the demonstration of independence, the level of questioning is important. Participants expressed regret that NEDs did not ask searching questions: Bernard Seaton expressed considerable dissatisfaction with the way the Runic audit committee operated and was particularly disappointed in the lack of questions: 'I think it was difficult for these people to understand the operational difficulties – they're not close to it, I don't think they understand the day-to-day problems at all.. so perhaps you wouldn't expect them to ask questions. Operationally they're not really up to speed with what is happening ..'

Two internal auditors suggested that, on occasion, they had managed the entire process: 'I identified the problem – and the solution - for them' (Simon Middleton, Glengarry), 'I think we came up with a solution before they asked' (Robin Dunston, Scrimshaw). This confirms the argument advanced in chapter 5 that the meeting itself may represent a ceremonial process, most of the substantive activity having taken place elsewhere. This is hardly surprising when one considers the brief to be fulfilled by audit committees (Cadbury Committee, 1992:73-4) in the context of a total meeting time per year which averages seven hours (Collier, 1992:81).

Regret at a limited level of questioning may appear to contradict the assumption that executive directors wish to influence NEDs but possibly indicates that demonstration of the capacity to cope with more searching questions is of value to finance directors. Chris Tracker spoke proudly of previous experience as finance director at a company where '..it [the audit committee] was much much tougher......we had Sir John Harvey-Jones, Sir Colin Marshall, Sir David Simon and Dick Giordano..'

The satisfactory handling of searching questions from individuals of such standing in the business world reflects well on all concerned, enhancing reputations: again, a ceremonial performance may be discerned. Although the content of the questions was not explained, it seems unlikely that questions would be designed purely to seek information since most participants described the possibility of 'information overload' (see section 6.1). The performance of questioning is as important, for both questioner and those providing answers, as the information conveyed. The audit committee provides an arena for NEDs to demonstrate their independence: '..I think most problems are because people just don't read the papers or they're not inclined to ask the next question after they've read the papers... he[a member of the audit committee] is tremendously useful and a real bulldozer, he really gives the management a hard time on occasion...you sit round the [Runic] board you hear [him] at great length... (Henry Morton)

There is a hint here of a slightly antagonistic personality tolerated because audit committee participants and board members derive some reassurance from this behaviour: this person can be relied upon to ask the 'difficult' questions that others might shy away from. However, this demonstration will take place within constraints.

The process of iteration will also be conditioned by the need for the NED to maintain his or her own position. Finch (1992:199) commented: 'Apart from any lack of independence, a non-executive director's eagerness to probe .. may be tempered by a perceived need to relate constructively to executive directors and to avoid 'being seen as a nuisance'.'

Spencer (1983:41) also observed: 'The 'awkward questions', it seems, must be asked 'non-abrasively', but also in a manner sufficiently skilful to obtain answers. There would seem to be rather a precise question of balance involved there, in that: '..there is the point that asking too many awkward questions may cause you to be regarded with disfavour and even removed from the board.''

The response of those required to provide answers – usually the finance director or internal auditor – may range from a resigned tolerance of being 'led down blind alleys because they've read something in the papers or this is happening down the road' (Robin Dunston, Scrimshaw) to an enthusiasm for a genuine and helpful interest expressed through questions: '..you want an effective audit committee which means that if the finance director knows they understand accounts, he will do a better job too - it all moves on to a higher plane..' (Roy Milford, Harrier)

The asking of questions and receipt of a response is part of a complex interaction. Either the initial answer is considered to be satisfactory when measured against some unspecified yardstick (for example, are we convinced by this person's account?) or unsatisfactory, in which case more reassurance would be demanded through an iterative and possibly negotiated process until an appropriate level of consensus about satisfaction was reached. At the extreme, if consensus cannot be reached, the audit committee member may opt to resign from the board: '.. there was an entrepreneurial chairman ... there was no audit committee. It was a public company, I insisted upon an audit committee and we worked it a couple of times and then I found that, yes, things came out of the audit committee but things came out that should have been brought to the board before and I felt very uncomfortable about it. I felt that the communication wasn't right and I resigned from the board.' (Henry Morton)

The point at which a NED will appear to be satisfied with answers received will probably vary according to the level of perceived risk in the issue involved. Henry believed that the risk to his reputation was such that resignation was his only option although he indicated that this was by no means an easy decision: '..you know one looks back and thinks 'Should there have been some other thing that one should have done?' and I decided no, there were shareholders interests, the shareholders were best served by my simply doing that - because one could create a tremendous furore, share price collapses and God knows what, what have you achieved by that? It was a perfectly well run company, it had got good management, it was just that they weren't complying with what one felt they should do and the fact that there was this one chairman with a lot of shares who still treated the company as his own..'

Part or all of this questioning process may take place within the formal audit committee meeting but participants' accounts indicated that much of the committee's activity took place outside meetings and centred on the audit committee chairman who appears to take on a greater responsibility than other members: '..as a chairman I talk about the agenda and the papers beforehand and suggest directions that it might go particularly in the internal audit side and I run through the judgements and the presentation format if you like of the accounts beforehand so that I'm prepared. As I say, other members of the audit committee probably just turn up on the day having leafed through the papers..' (Max Tinker, Runic)

Asking the right questions and interpreting the answers appropriately is made possible by the experience and knowledge of the NEDs: participants believed that NEDs required a general business background to be effective and that the audit committee should include one person with sufficient technical expertise to grasp accounting issues, who may be expected to ensure that the process generates an appropriate level of comfort for all concerned: 'You also need someone who is frankly the sort of person who will read all the papers very carefully - you know, there's no doubt that the finance guy will read the detailed notes to the accounts and think through the implications and connotations of what's said in a way that's different to somebody who hasn't got that finance background' (Alex Anderson, Glengarry)

The process was summed up by Robin Dunston: 'They [the audit committee members] are conscious of their responsibilities and lack of knowledge of the day to day running of the business – [they are] feeling their way in terms of information required and what sort of reassurance they want from us.. they just want to be sure that the company is addressing control issues seriously and that's what they're finding their way towards, that comfort..'

The questioning process may thus be viewed as a means by which audit committee members can demonstrate their independence of mind. The outcome of the process will normally be a carefully managed consensus about issues raised – a confirmation that audit committee members are reassured by the responses provided. This will be reported to the main board who will be similarly reassured that the audit committee has dealt with the matter on their behalf. Thus the independence of audit committee members is performed in the audit committee meeting by a process of questioning: it is produced as a commodity which enhances the value of consensus by demonstrating that the parties involved have arrived at agreement without coercion or influence, through a process of logical debate and rational judgement.

8.5 INDEPENDENCE AS A COMMODITY AND AS AN INTERESSEMENT DEVICE

Williams (1992:106) suggested that independence may be viewed as a commodity: 'Independence no longer refers to a virtue possessed by *a* practitioner; it is now a commodity disembodied from any particular practitioner at all... Independence is no longer something to be committed to, no longer something that *is*; it is now something one calculates.'

Both conceptions of independence that Williams described appear within the accounts of participants: while they emphasise the importance of independence of mind, there is also a sense in which independence may be seen as a commodity in the context of audit committee activity. Independence is 'produced' within the framework of audit committee activity through the independence of connection of its members, demonstrated through the formal selection process and limits to tenure, and their independence of mind, demonstrated through their behaviour in the questioning process. It is then 'supplied' by the audit committee to the main board, to the external auditors and to users of financial statements, as a component of 'comfort ' (discussed in detail in chapter 9).

At a broader level the demonstration of independence becomes an interessement device, giving the company the opportunity to mobilise resources: Tsui et al (1994) demonstrated that bankers would more readily advance loans where they perceived that auditor independence was assured by the existence of an audit committee.

This chapter has discussed the importance of independence within the Cadbury perspective and within the stories of audit committee participants. It has suggested that an important role for independence lies in the validation of consensus, and has highlighted the ceremonial aspect of questioning by audit committee members as a demonstration of independence.

The process may be represented thus:

INDEPENDENCE

is a personal quality of audit committee members demonstrated by

QUESTIONING

leading through iterations to a validated

CONSENSUS

about appropriateness of responses

The next chapter further develops the relationship between consensus validated by independence and the production of comfort.

Chapter 9
COMFORT

Chapters 7 and 8 identified the audit committee's achievement of consensus, validated by perceptions of its independence, as a means of generating comfort. This chapter explores participants' use of the word 'comfort' and associated expressions and suggests that comfort is a commodity which is passed to and from the audit committee. Generation of comfort is proposed as an important but unarticulated role of the audit committee, as it is for the audit process itself, giving the financial reports authenticity which legitimises the company and allows its continuing existence through access to resources.

9.1 THE COMFORTING ROLE OF AUDIT

'Auditing has the character of a certain kind of organizational script whose dramaturgical essence is the production of comfort.' (Power, 1997:123)

The notion of comfort as a commodity was identified by Pentland (1993) in an examination of the audit process. He asserted that the role of auditors is to: '..give 'comfort' to people who are vulnerable to erroneous, self-interested, and possibly fraudulent statements from corporate management.' (1993:606)

Pentland then examined how 'comfort' was created, through his observation of audit teams at work and interviews with members of the teams and other auditors. Within the audit activity he identified processes of purification, social control and impression management which give audit a ritual nature. He noted the use of the concept of comfort in the language used by those he observed and interviewed, concluding that: 'Objectively, unaudited numbers may be risky or uncertain, but subjectively, they make auditors feel uncomfortable. Audit rituals make them 'comfortable' by transforming and purifying the inherently 'unclean' client data.' (1993:609)

Pentland suggested that the process of 'getting comfortable' was based on a 'series of repeated interactions with members of the team' and that comfort thus became a commodity that could be passed on to other individuals, changing from an emotional state shared between individuals and eventually becoming 'an objective, institutionalised fact[57] as it is passed on via the audit report to the public: 'The audit opinion found in every annual report constitutes the paradigm example of comfort as a commodity' (1993:611)

Pentland thus demonstrated how: '..micro-interactions within the engagement team create comfort, which makes the macro-order of capital markets and other financial institutions possible..' (Pentland, 1993:606)

The stories of audit committee participants indicate that interactions in and around the audit committee perform a very similar function of comfort generation and exchange.

9.2   THE AUDIT COMMITTEE AS A SEEKER OF COMFORT

The words 'comfort' and 'comfortable' were used frequently by interviewees, as were similar expressions such as 'reassured by' and 'happy with'. The network of comfort provision traced in the stories of participants is complex: comfort is provided both to and by the audit committee. The audit committee initially seeks comfort: 'I think because of the complexities they [the audit committee] just want to make sure that - on a face to face - that everyone makes sure that they are absolutely happy with what's going on.' (Ronald Roberts)

In chapter 5 the physical environment and timing of the audit committee meeting were examined as interessement/enrolment devices used by participants to strengthen their networks. The usefulness of these devices depends on the level of comfort generated. Part of the process of achieving comfort relates to the physical environment of the meeting. Seating arrangements may add important emphasis to issues of status and influence among members of the committee: '..he knows he's not on the audit committee but he sits on the side of the table where the audit committee are and just to confuse matters we've now got one member of the audit committee who sits on the other side..'(Max Tinker, Runic) - a strategy which Max viewed as designed to induce discomfort among participants.

Audit committees normally meet in the board room or its equivalent, usually in a setting of considerable physical comfort (except perhaps in the more crowded circumstances described by Roy Milford at Harrier, quoted in section 6.2), often designed to emphasise the status of the board and its members. The comfort of the environment thus contributes to the generation of comfort by the audit committee, an additional enrolment device employed by those participants 'managing' the meeting.

Further comfort is provided by the security of habit: participants' stories indicated that those attending the meetings usually sat in the same place each time, often the same place as they would sit for main board meetings: '..it's the comfort of sitting in same place at meetings.' (Alex Anderson, Glengarry) '. I think people feel comfortable knowing that that is the situation but I don't think there would be a terrible trauma if someone sat in a different place.' (Henry Morton, Runic)

The timing of the meeting, discussed in section 6.2, is also important in generating comfort: if the audit committee immediately precedes the main board meeting – a logistically convenient arrangement – there may be considerable pressure on the audit committee to complete its business in time to report to the subsequent board meeting. Max Tinker and Chris Scrimshaw both observed that a time gap was more comfortable for those participants required to provide information:

'..if there are changes, and there might be a change for example to the dividend recommendation, so if there are changes and there's often changes in the drafting, not necessarily in the numbers or the notes but in the chairman's report, so it enables us to print those and get a book proof to the board, if it's the finals anyway, so really it's giving us a little gap. Also it enables us to produce the minutes so that the full board have the minutes of the audit committee meeting and the chairman of the audit committee time to think what he's going to report. Now all those things are possible in twenty four hours or overnight but they're more comfortable [if there is a time gap]' (Max Tinker, Runic)

'.. he [the audit committee chair] used to quite like having it in the morning like nine o'clock, the board starts at ten, something like that, but, after about two years, we began to realise that it was totally impractical, we didn't get the assurance that we needed if there were issues.. I couldn't rush out in two minutes and get the answer.' (Chris Tracker, Scrimshaw)

Comfort is provided to the audit committee by the finance director and internal auditor through the iterative questioning process discussed in chapter 8. Finance directors described how they would manage this process: '..[the internal audit] programme as well is significant because behind that is their risk analysis so there's a discussion on that where people will say 'Well, I thought that (let's say) your foreign exchange hedging was a big risk - why doesn't that appear very high?' and the internal auditor will explain why he graded it low and I will say 'Well, it's all under control, as you know'.' (Max Tinker) '.. the chairman of the audit committee and the others would say 'What are we doing about this? It's been raised as an issue now, I don't want to see it there again' - we need to say that we're going to sort it...(Chris Tracker)

The context of these stories and the manner in which they were recounted suggested that the process of questioning was a necessary formality, further emphasising the ceremonial aspect of the audit committee meeting. The questions posed by audit committee members were not sufficiently penetrating to address the underlying issues in a way that challenged the respondents to any great extent and the questioners could be satisfied with comforting comments such as 'It's all under control' and 'We're going to sort it'.

At Scrimshaw, Robin Dunston, the internal auditor described the process in greater detail: '.. they're looking for, you know, 'What recommendations have we made that haven't been put in? What are the main outstanding issues?' - this sort of thing, which is fine but I'm not sure I've yet got them quite to understand the range of work we cover, the sorts of things we come up with and how its progressed in the business and they're almost taking a simplistic view.. you know they're talking about financial risk here .. 'The auditors have said do this, ..the Barings factor comes into this …. these are being done, we've said do it, it doesn't happen, why hasn't [Chris Tracker, the finance director] made them do it?' Usually there's a degree of greyness about it, these are big issues but then they're not just pure financial risk, these are largely often operational things.'

The distinction Robin makes between financial risk and business risk is an important one, echoed by Bob Cunningham who emphasised that the role of the audit committee should be confined to issues of financial risk. However, the two types of risk may be very difficult to disentangle and the

150

ambiguity of the NED's dual role, as a monitor of fellow executive directors and also as a director brought in to contribute broad business skills to board activity, adds further complexity. Robin's account suggests that NEDs find it difficult to understand that financial risks cannot be addressed in isolation since the consequences of measures taken for their minimisation may increase general business risks. The balance between the two types of risk needs to be explained carefully to ensure that comfort is still maintained.

Comfort levels will also be threatened by external factors: Robin referred to the 'Barings factor' and Chris Tracker indicated the problems which are raised by NEDs' experience of the 'nasty surprise' in other companies: 'It got very emotional at the last one [audit committee meeting] when we were talking about technical requirements, obviously internal control, partly because the non-execs had been at other audit committees where the year end had perhaps been the calendar year end, so the discussion had taken place a few weeks earlier where they were talking about getting independent advice... It was a discussion rather than a criticism - how are we going to handle it?'

'Internal control' is a reference to a particularly problematic area of the Cadbury recommendations: the recommendation that 'directors should make a statement on the effectiveness of internal controls and that the auditors should report thereon.' (Cadbury Committee, 1992:27). Response to this was generally unfavourable as criteria for assessing effectiveness were unclear and there was general concern about the possibility of subsequent litigation based on such reports. Power (1997:56) noted that the controversy about this requirement illustrated 'the problems of an indirect regulatory style' since: '..a certain chain of empty opinions substitutes for information and can be created by auditors forming an opinion about the opinion of directors.'

Glengarry, however, was one of the few companies which chose to report unequivocally in this area: this is discussed below in section 9.4.[58]

Reassurance on internal control may be sought from the internal audit function: '..[audit committee members are] conscious of their responsibilities and lack of knowledge of the day to day running of the business – feeling their way in terms of information required and what sort of reassurance they want from us....they just want to be sure that the company is addressing control issues seriously and that's what they're finding their way towards, that comfort – all that means it's becoming a more serious committee, it realises its responsibilities and is thinking about how it can handle them.'(Robin Dunston at Scrimshaw)

However, at Runic the relationship between the audit committee and the internal auditor was rather different, as illustrated by Bernard Seaton's story of expressing concerns to the audit committee that were not followed up:

'I feel and have expressed the view that the audit committee and the board ought to be asking for me to do more work in terms of compliance. There's been a board decision based on <u>this</u> data to achieve <u>this</u> objective - in six months time you want your internal audit to go and audit the factual outturn of that information that was given to the board. Now I think that's what they ought to be doing but that isn't something that happens.. I wouldn't say they take the initiative – I'm giving them the initiative. I'm giving them the bullets to fire if you like ....I think they're reactive .. they have very little operational knowledge of the business. I think Cadbury really is asking them to do things that they're not trying or have the experience to undertake..'

In Bernard's view, the Runic audit committee were excessively complacent and were ignoring areas of risk about which they should have expressed more concern. Bernard had been unsuccessful in enrolling the audit committee to achieve his objectives. Ronald Roberts revealed that there was some difference of opinion on the value of internal audit within the committee, but ascribed the lack of apparent interest on the part of the audit committee to their confidence in Bernard:

'..one has to say that there are certain people that are not desperately keen on internal audit, certain non executives who genuinely don't see a huge value out of internal audit, and others who see a lot of value and there is that mix and I think that's the difficulty that [Bernard] faces..the way they look at it in a lot of ways is 'Are we happy with the general breadth of what he's doing and the depth of what he's doing? Then leave it up to him highlight by exception those issues which he wants to discuss with us'.. I think they have confidence in [Bernard].. if he feels there's an issue to be debated, he's not going to stand on ceremony, he will put it down so, from that point of view you know that's a positive side, it's not as if someone's saying, well he's not allowed to say things, from that point of view he's entirely independent..'

Bernard's behaviour had, however, antagonised Henry Morton, the audit committee chairman: when referring to Bernard, Henry pointedly called him 'Seaton' whereas all other individuals were referred to by their first names. '.. [Seaton] produces all the reports - sometimes the odd point which perhaps he thinks in his view is important but which we might not weigh the same importance to - now I think one of the things which he felt very strongly about and it's almost outside of the audit committee's terms of reference59, was on audit fees where he thought that the audit fees were too high. I think he felt that internal audit were doing certain things to replace the work and here were the auditors coming along and wanting a big jump in their fees. It may be no secret to you to know that [XYZ] when they won the audit at [Runic] quoted substantially lower than their predecessors but three or four years later I can well understand why they wanted to increase the fees so that was an area where [Seaton] was being really quite aggressive saying 'Here am I doing all this, how can they justify it?' and was possibly a bit disappointed - we were in a much more compromising role and felt the audit fee, although it was high and we'd challenge it, I think on the whole we felt we were getting value for money. I am not one who likes to squeeze professional fees too tightly, although I don't like paying too much - there is a point where you start reducing the fees, you start reducing the service..'

Bernard was dismissive of the audit committee and emphasised that, although he reported to the finance director, he was also in direct communication with those he considered to be the more important members of the board: '..I need to know that they [chairman of company and chief executive] are comfortable - the audit committee is only the agent of the board. I do make a point of going to see them both, really as a comfort test as far as I'm concerned.' (Bernard Seaton, Runic)

There is a sense in these stories that Bernard, not a member of the audit committee, was almost performing the monitoring role expected of a non executive director. This may have been useful in terms of initiating a form of 'constrained dissension' within audit committee meetings that would serve as a demonstration of independence, in a similar way to that performed by the American NED on the Runic board (see sections 5.1, 7.2, 8.4). Both individuals were clearly unpopular, standing outside the friendly relationships described in chapter 7: their unsuccessful attempts at enrolment could be seen as strengthening the network of which they were not a part. The fact that these individuals were raising issues for discussion provided a form of reassurance to the committee because the discussion offered an opportunity to demonstrate concern about the issues, even if, as Bernard believed, the concern was not followed by appropriate action. Audit committee members could also derive comfort from a display of their own tolerance.

In contrast, the internal auditors at Scrimshaw and Glengarry were clearly skilled at creating comfort through their interactions with the audit committee, particularly in managing the questioning process, as noted in chapter 8.

A further external source of discomfort may be pronouncements by the Accounting Standards Board which need explanation. Such pronouncements are often fairly technical and audit committee members may need reassurance about their implementation. Here comfort may be provided to the audit committee by the external auditor in his/her capacity as expert advisor : '..when we've had controversial issues, which we have had, it's been quite important that in the end the [external auditor] partner says well yes, having warned us about being reported to the FRC[60] and all this nonsense, that in the end what we're doing is acceptable and proper..'(Roy Milford, Harrier). '..the chairman of the committee can turn to [XYZ] and say 'Are you satisfied with this approach?' and that gives the chairman a lot of comfort that it has been looked at.' (Bernard Seaton, Runic)

Comfort may also be generated internally within the audit committee, for example to the chair through the status and calibre of the other non-executive directors: '..I think he drew some comfort from the fact that he had some fairly important non executive directors around him - not including me, I was one of the less important... plenty of double barrelled names with lots of ministerial and other experience..' (Henry Morton, Runic)

At what level will audit committee members feel comfortable? Presumably at the point at which the iterations of the questioning process described in chapter 8 reassure them that the risk of 'nasty surprises' has been contained. Resignation from the board will be the ultimate expression of discomfort as noted in Henry Morton's story in section 8.4.

The audit committee thus seeks comfort from the specific characteristics of meetings such as the physical environment, seating arrangements and timing, from the status and background of other members and from the finance director and internal auditor through the questioning process examined in chapter 8.

9.3   THE AUDIT COMMITTEE AS A PROVIDER OF COMFORT

Having been 'made comfortable', the audit committee is then in a position to act as a comfort provider. It provides comfort for finance directors and internal auditors through its support over internal control issues, as discussed in 5.5. There is no doubt that this audit committee role can be immensely helpful in problematic areas of internal control - for example, in industries where long term research and development investment is crucial to success but difficult to monitor where cultures of innovation and control clash: '..internal audit say constantly we don't control [Y division] adequately from a financial and administrative control point of view and I just say in passing that there's the issue of when people are innovative and so on.. you have a balance between stopping the innovation with the control or controlling them without them running out of control at the other side.'(Max Tinker, Runic)

As well as demonstrating to the world at large that the external auditors are independent from management influence, there is evidence that external auditors themselves derive comfort from the existence of the audit committee (Beattie et al, 1997) although none interviewed referred explicitly to this. The audit committee offers a means of enhancing the appearance of auditor independence at no cost to the auditor (Eichenseher and Shields,1985) and in situations of crisis over company reporting the existence of an audit committee may divert allegations of blame away from the external auditor.

The audit committee provides comfort to the main board through its specialist focus on delegated tasks: '..key reports that are done are shared with the executive directors who don't attend, so it's also if you like a bit of comfort for them.' (Chris Tracker, Scrimshaw)   '..with this particular item last year.. the chairman of the audit committee would have reported it to the board that there was this issue, it had been discussed, there were these two alternatives, this is what had been decided.. he's reporting to the board so the board are aware of the decision that's been made...you can't spend board meetings going through stuff the audit committee has already been through.' (Alex Anderson, Glengarry)

However, as noted in section 6.1, Samuels et al (1996) reported contradictory evidence, citing executive directors who were unhappy that they were no longer fully informed on audit matters. Clearly, they had not

155

been provided with a sufficient level of comfort to believe that the audit committee was undertaking its delegated tasks appropriately: since all directors are equally liable, their concern is understandable.

Chris Tracker suggested that the view of the executive directors could be summed up thus: '..the accounts are signed off and as long as the people who've signed them are happy, the auditor's happy, the finance director's happy, you know it's not really our problem.'

The ritual importance of the audit 'signing off' process in generating comfort was observed by Pentland (1993). The final signing of the company accounts performs a similar function: the published statements will be used as an interessement/enrolment device to confirm the status of the company in the eyes of providers of finance. Comfort is thus passed on to external users of company accounts.

9.4   THE MAINTENANCE OF COMFORT LEVELS

This analysis demonstrates that the audit committee will itself receive comfort from various sources and will then be able to transmit it to others. The notion of comfort as a commodity implies some concept of its value. ' You assess effectiveness from the perspective of process - does the system work? - and outputs – the lack of surprises, the degree of comfort..'(Ken Palmer)

Different perceived levels and sources of risk may require different levels of comfort generation; participants' stories indicate a continuing preoccupation with the provision and maintenance of comfort. Comfort is emotional and has a certain fragility that may be swiftly undermined: the network of relationships among audit committee participants requires a level of 'maintenance' in order to support the generation of comfort.

At Glengarry, the recent controversial history meant that comfort was a priority, in terms of the public image of the company, as indicated by Alex Anderson:

'I think that it - firstly because of what happened, that was a catalyst to change and therefore there was a lot of change in terms of people which meant that we could bring in a lot of very good people. Secondly, there was a clear recognition that we needed to be very strong on controls and also very strong on corporate governance and controls are an important part of that and I think that the further point there is, in terms of financial reporting, that seems one way to demonstrate our commitment to high standards - to always have a very high standard of financial reporting and that would obviously depend on a number of areas and I think now we attempt to always represent best practice but not necessarily to be leading the field. So I think, you know, that the history has made it much easier for people to get focussed on internal control and for the senior management to recognise that internal controls are important. One obviously focuses very much on how to make money for shareholders but that's all very well but you've actually got to have the right controls and the right framework in place so that not only do you make money but you do it in the proper way, you don't lose it for them....we are responsible for our accounts, the auditors are there to audit them and it's a much harder challenge for us to be comfortable that we're doing things the right way, than it is to convince the auditors that we're doing it right and I think that's a very important point to make, and one that I do make to the directors. You know it's not a matter of convincing the auditors to accept some sort of sporty treatment but actually are <u>we</u> comfortable that it is the right treatment?'

The replacement of the board which led Glengarry into crisis by directors such as Martin Johnson, with established reputations for probity and experience of 'turning round' companies in crisis, was very important. A demonstrable commitment to high standards of corporate governance was also essential. Note Alex's comment about not necessarily 'leading the field' in financial reporting practice: the company's image - and the comfort of potential finance providers - could be compromised by the suggestion that the reports were based on creative accounting practices or 'sporty treatments'. The company did not want to be seen as being in any way controversial. However, the board opted to report on internal control effectiveness, an issue that had caused some difficulties at other companies, as noted in section 9.2. Any concerns about potential liability from such statements were presumably outweighed by the benefits of being perceived as keen to disclose such information, particularly when other companies had proved reluctant to do so. The use of the terms 'right' and 'proper' also highlights Alex's concern to present the company appropriately.

Participants' stories demonstrated that comfort is generated and maintained within the ceremonial framework of the audit committee. However, there may be dangers associated with comfort generation, as identified by writers such as Janis (1985) who introduced the concept of 'groupthink', Gersick and Hackman (1990) in their examination of the effects on performance of 'habitual routines', and Harvey's notion of the 'Abilene paradox' (Harvey, 1988). A desire to conform to group norms, to 'fit in', may prevent audit committee members from raising difficult questions and challenging assumptions that appear to be widely held. The 'irritant' provided by difficult personalities, such as Bernard Seaton at Runic discussed in section 9.2, and Martin Johnson at Glengarry, serves a useful purpose: the behaviour of these individuals serves to demonstrate the independence of the audit committee, while saving other members from jeopardising their own position within the group[61]. Bailey's analysis of committees characterised the 'senile' committee as follows: 'The committee meetings become ritual performances; no new kinds of information are accepted because the received wisdom comprises all that is needed; and the committee is incapable of doing anything that it has not done before.' (1983:115-6)

Part of the role of the independent NED is presumably to ensure that this stagnation does not happen, that the committee does not become so comfortable that it falls into an unquestioned pattern of consensual behaviour. Alex Anderson certainly viewed the independence of NEDs as a factor enabling them to restrain misguided enthusiasm: 'I think from the point of view of the company there is no doubt that non executives do bring an added dimension. They are, you know, because they are independent, they are able to deal with people getting a bit over enthusiastic, to say 'Hang on a second guys, let's be sensible about this' so I think, you know, it does work..'

Henry Morton had a similar view, describing the effect on the Runic chairman of non executive appointments in other companies: '..particularly if you're in good quality companies, and he is, and I can see he comes back and he wants to introduce some of these things he's seen and sometimes the non execs say, you know, 'Good idea!', others say 'For God's sake, that's too avant garde, let's leave somebody else to take the lead on that!' but it's caused him to bring up issues that he would never have known about probably..'

9.5   COMFORT AS A COMMODITY

Comfort is generated within the interactions within and around the audit committee. Chapter 6 examined the ways in which participants use the ceremonial devices of the audit committee meeting as interessement and enrolment devices: these manoeuvres may all be seen as 'comfort generators' since enrolment depends in part on comfort. Actors will be enrolled in networks if they believe that such enrolment will make them feel comfortable to a degree that will encourage them to abandon other enrolments.

Pentland's discussion of comfort generation in the audit process uses Collins' theory of interaction ritual chains. Collins (1981) developed the concept of 'interaction ritual chains' to demonstrate the link between micro and macro levels of sociological analysis. He suggested that: 'Such chains of micro-encounter generate the central features of social organization...by creating and recreating "mythical" cultural symbols and emotional energies.'(1981:985)

He argued that aspects of social structure such as property and authority are ultimately based on individuals' 'feelings of membership in coalitions' and that any explanation of social structure should therefore answer the questions: 'What makes someone a member of a coalition? What determines the extensiveness of a coalition and the intensity of bonds within it? How do people judge the power of coalitions?' (1981:998)

These are similar questions to those explored by Callon's 'moments of translation', discussed in chapter 4, and the analysis of network formation through the processes of problematisation, interessement, enrolment and mobilisation goes some way to answering them.

Collins focused on the individual interaction ritual of conversation which he characterised as an exchange of emotional and cultural resources which have been acquired by the participants from previous exchanges, leading to the concept of the 'interaction ritual chain' through which such resources are constituted at macro level into the social structure. Using this approach, Pentland (1993) demonstrated that comfort, an emotional resource, is generated within the audit team through micro interactions and is then passed on within the audit firm and ultimately to the general public. In a similar way, this chapter has demonstrated how comfort is generated within the audit committee through the interactions between members and other participants, and is then passed on to the main board and ultimately to the users of the financial statements presented by the directors.

The relationship between independence, consensus and comfort may now be summarised as follows:

INDEPENDENCE

is a personal quality of audit committee members demonstrated by

QUESTIONING

leading through iterations to a validated

CONSENSUS

about appropriateness of responses, which generates

COMFORT

transmitted to main board and users of financial statements

From an ANT perspective:

INDEPENDENCE demonstrated through **QUESTIONING** facilitates the interessement and enrolment of audit committee members, validating the **CONSENSUS** which represents the mobilisation or punctualisation stage, leading to **COMFORT**, a resource generated within the network, which is of value to other networks (the main board, external resource providers) and thus strengthens the network within which it is produced.

9.6   COMFORT AND LEGITIMACY

In the context of audit committee activity, the principal purpose of comfort generation is reassurance about perceived levels of risk. Comfort is provided to the audit committee:
- by the finance director and internal auditor who supply information about systems and processes designed to minimise risk. This information may be supplied directly or elicited through questioning. Other members of company management may be asked to provide further information in specific areas.
- by the external auditor in his/her role as expert in technical accounting matters.
- by its own members' status, skills and experience.

Comfort is provided by the audit committee:
- to the finance director and internal auditor as a support in implementing internal control procedures.
- to the main board by reporting on the accomplishment of delegated tasks.

Comfort is then passed on by the board of directors to the external users of financial statements: the public report of the existence and activity of the audit committee boosts confidence that the company has high standards of corporate governance, reassuring resource providers.

The existence and activity of the audit committee thus confirms the belief that standards of financial reporting quality are adequate (to prevent 'nasty surprises') but within the existing framework of financial reporting there is no independently verifiable measure of such quality, as Wolnizer (1995) has observed. There is, however, some evidence that engendering this belief may be sufficient to permit companies to access resources. Tsui et al (1994) demonstrated that bankers perceived a lower loan risk when given information on the presence of audit committees as a result of increased confidence in auditor independence. Felton et al (1996:170) reported a survey which indicated that investors would pay a premium of up to 16% for investments in companies which they perceived to have good governance, for the following reasons:

'Some believe that a company with good governance will perform better over time, leading to a higher stock price.. Other see good governance as a means of reducing risk, as they believe that it decreases the likelihood of bad things happening to a company. Also, when bad things do happen, they expect well-governed companies to rebound more quickly. Still others regard the recent increase in attention to governance as a fad. However, they tag along because so many investors do value governance. As this group sees it, the stock of a well-governed company may be worth more simply because governance is such a hot topic these days.'

Coombes and Watson (2000) surveyed institutional investors in Asia, Europe, the United States and Latin America during 1999-2000 and identified premiums ranging from 18% to 28%. They commented: '..companies that fail to reform their governance will find themselves at a competitive disadvantage when they try to obtain capital to finance growth.' (2000:77).Thus the demonstration of concern with good governance appears to generate comfort among both investors and lenders with positive effects on a company's ability to raise finance.

A company's display of concern for high standards of corporate governance is facilitated by the demonstration of established internal monitoring procedures. The role of monitoring procedures as a symbol of legitimacy has been noted by writers such as Power (1997:14) who characterised 'the audit society' as a collection of: '..ritualised practices of verification whose technical efficacy is less significant than their role in the production of organizational legitimacy.'

Harrison (1987:113) commented, with particular reference to audit committees, that: 'Since it is very difficult to observe what work these committees actually do, however, there is the possibility that monitoring committees will be established to create a favourable appearance, but that they will do very little in terms of active oversight of the corporation's activities..'

Harrison's analysis drew on the work of DiMaggio and Powell (1983) who suggested that organisations introduce structural changes such as audit committees through a process of 'institutional isomorphism' which is designed to ensure legitimacy (and access to resources) through compliance with established norms:

'It is important to note that each of the institutional isomorphic processes can be expected to proceed in the absence of evidence that they increase internal organizational efficiency. To the extent that organizational effectiveness is enhanced, the reason will often be that organizations are rewarded for being similar to other organizations in their fields. This similarity can make it easier for organizations to transact with other organizations, to attract career-minded staff, to be acknowledged as legitimate and reputable, and to fit into administrative categories that define eligibility for public and private grants and contracts. None of this, however, insures that conformist organizations do what they do more efficiently than their deviant peers.' (1983:153-4)[2]

Institutional theory thus offers a possible explanation for Collier's 'curious phenomenon' of audit committee establishment. More recently, Kalbers and Fogarty (1996) observed that: 'The formal empowerment of the audit committee appears to be designed for the consumption of external parties with some interest in the adherence to adequate forms of corporate control... This study suggests that changes in the structure of corporate governance may be primarily symbolic..' (1996:26-7)

The empirical data reported in this study provides further confirmation of the suggestions of Kalbers and Fogarty. The generation of comfort is revealed as an important but unarticulated role of the audit committee, suggesting that an important aspect of audit committee operation may be the level of comfort generated – the confidence that there will be no nasty surprises. The generation of comfort may thus provide a partial explanation for the apparently unjustified popularity of audit committees – Collier's 'curious phenomenon'.

This chapter has demonstrated that the notions of independence, consensus and comfort are central to the operations of the audit committee. The level of comfort generated within these operations acts as an interessement/enrolment device, persuading parties external to the company that high standards of corporate governance are being maintained, supporting the company's claim to legitimacy and facilitating its access to resources from external parties.

Chapter 10
CONCLUSION

This study has argued that an important and unacknowledged role of the audit committee is the provision of comfort, through a process of ceremonial performance. A model of this process has been drawn out of the accounts of audit committee participants, using an analytical framework derived from actor-network theory. The comfort thus generated supports claims to organizational legitimacy and facilitates resource access. The study offers a possible explanation for the popularity of audit committees despite their apparent lack of effectiveness in improving corporate governance standards. This chapter reviews the research process, considers recent corporate governance developments in the US and the UK and their effect on audit committees and suggests areas for future research.

10.1 REFLECTIONS ON THE RESEARCH PROCESS

As noted in chapter 1, the study was envisaged as an investigation of the role of the audit committee. The original research question evolved from a broad consideration of:

- what is an audit committee, how does it work and what makes it effective?

to:

- what does audit committee effectiveness mean to audit committee participants?

This was the outcome of initial data analysis which highlighted the contrast between the rhetoric about the value of the audit committee as a corporate governance mechanism, as embodied in the Cadbury Code, and the scepticism expressed by those directly involved in audit committee work. Within the audit committee literature, an associated research question was identified:

- why have audit committees become so widely established in large UK public limited companies when evidence of their effectiveness is limited? – Collier's 'curious phenomenon' (Collier:1996).

The study was not intended to derive further prescriptions relating to audit committee activity in pursuit of the ideal 'effective' model. The review of the relevant literature in chapter 2 confirms that evidence of audit committee effectiveness is scarce. This scarcity is attributed in part to the lack of clarity about audit committee purpose, which makes it difficult to develop criteria whereby effectiveness might be assessed. This study suggests that the situated nature of understandings of effectiveness compounds the difficulties involved: it demonstrates that concepts of effectiveness are likely to vary between individuals, organizations, countries and over time, making generalised prescription inappropriate.

As well as demonstrating a shortage of evidence to substantiate audit committee effectiveness, the literature review has highlighted significant criticism of the potential for audit committees ever to be effective, in terms of their representation by Cadbury as a monitoring and control device. The assumptions that underpin the Cadbury Code have been questioned: the link between auditor independence and improved financial reporting quality appears tenuous and the definition of such quality is also obscure (Jonas and Blanchet, 2000). The use of a qualitative approach focuses attention on the fact that the practice of corporate governance involves people – people who operate within a complex pattern of relationships that may contradict and subvert such assumptions. This study thus supports the challenges presented by Grout et al (1994), Wolnizer (1995) and Power (1997), by highlighting the existence of networks linking audit committee participants in ways that may undermine accepted understandings of independence but do not overtly damage the symbolic representation of high standards of corporate governance to external parties.

As observed in chapter 2, the influence of the dynamics of the relationships operating among audit committee participants remains largely unrecognised in the assessment of audit committee 'effectiveness', which has focused on conformity with generalised prescriptions with regard to structure and process. The methodological approach of this study was therefore chosen to facilitate the exploration of the conceptions of the audit committee role, and its effectiveness within that context, held by individual audit committee participants. The inductive approach characteristic of grounded theory seemed most appropriate, given the desirability of using a qualitative approach, discussed in chapter 2, and the broadness of the original research question which suggested a need for flexibility in response to data collected.

The data collection process was constrained by access limitations: given such constraints, interviews offered the most appropriate method of gathering data, although the methodological critique of the interview process is noted in section 3.5. The questionnaires were not designed as formal survey instruments, and the data collected therein has not been separately analysed, although, since it provided the basis for discussion in the subsequent interviews, it has essentially been incorporated into the study. However, it is clear that the use of this approach, even within such limitations, has generated a rich source of data which has not previously been explored in the audit committee literature.

As data analysis through coding and the development of categories proceeded, a reading of the actor-network theory literature indicated that the ANT approach would offer an appropriate way of thinking about and describing audit committee activity. ANT focuses on the generation of power and influence within and between networks which form and re-form. The emphasis on performativity in ANT resonated with the categories derived from the data that were associated with 'performance', as discussed in chapter 5. The data analysis also revealed complex and dynamic relationships among audit committee participants which could be examined and contextualised through the use of the concept of translation. A further advantage of ANT is that its tools of analysis may be used at both macro and micro levels: section 4.5 explores the development of the Cadbury Code from an ANT perspective, providing a context for the micro analysis in subsequent chapters.

Since ANT recognises the precariousness and fragmentation of networks, as demonstrated in the examination of the debate over the disclosure issue at Runic in chapter 7, it offers a richer picture than other theoretical frameworks previously used in the audit committee literature. The assumptions of agency theory, for example, underpin a more rigid explanatory framework which does not encompass the influences of the shifting allegiances forged by individuals in everyday interaction.

The robustness of the major categories derived from the data − performance, consensus, independence and comfort − was determined through repeated interplay with the data. The use of the ANT concept of translation facilitated a theorisation of the relationships between these categories. Against the background of the audit committee meeting, providing simultaneously an arena for the problematisation of issues and a ceremonial performance employed by participants as an interessement/enrolment device, the process of comfort generation is traced. The independence of participants is demonstrated through the key role of the performance of questioning, and independence is essential to the comfort value of consensus reached by the audit committee and main board. The acquisition of legitimacy is intimately connected to the provision of comfort through the formal report of audit committee existence and activity in published financial statements.

ANT is an evolving paradigm which has been subjected to both external criticism (eg Collins and Yearley, 1992) and internal criticism from its proponents (eg Law,1997). Those using ANT as a theoretical framework to examine accounting issues have been selective. Robson (1991) studied the development of the UK accounting standard setting programme using the concept of problematisation but did not make use of the more detailed framework of 'moments of translation'. Chua (1995) analysed the introduction of an accounting system – the development of a 'fact-building network' – using the ANT concept of inscription and explicitly rejecting the presentation of inanimate objects as actors. Ezzamel (1994) traced the individual stages of problematisation, interessement, enrolment and mobilisation in the contested situation of an attempt to introduce a budgeting system within a university. Many ANT studies are based on a series of events surrounding a specific and well-documented contest: both Ezzamel and Chua used ANT to frame individual case studies of situations where accounting systems were implicated in change which was resisted and both had privileged access to data as participants in the processes analysed.

This study has been similarly selective with regard to analytical tools but has attempted to use the identification of 'moments of translation' in three different ways:

- to analyse relationships among audit committee participants as networks form and re-form
- to explore the performative role of the audit committee meeting as an arena for problematisation as well as an interessement and enrolment device used by audit committee participants
- to explain the roles of independence, consensus and comfort as interessement and enrolment devices that strengthen the audit committee as a punctualisation of varied interests

One particular problem was encountered in using the concept of 'moments of translation' as an analytic tool. Ezzamel (1994:225) noted that 'the devices of interessement per se do not guarantee successful enrolment.' But the distinction between interessement and enrolment, while theoretically clear, was not always easy to observe within the data collected for this study. The actual process of enrolment may be obscure and enrolment may only be observable from subsequent behaviour in situations where, unlike those studied by Ezzamel and Chua, extensive and accessible documentation does not exist. This does not invalidate the applicability of the approach in this study since the focus is less on the occurrence of interessement or enrolment but rather on the devices employed to achieve them and there is no theoretical reason why the same device may not be used for both purposes.

The study thus contributes to the existing audit committee literature in the following important respects:

- it uses the theoretical approach of actor-network theory which has not previously been employed in the study of audit committees
- it presents a qualitative examination of the role of the audit committee in large UK public limited ompanies, which has not previously been attempted
- it confirms the thesis that audit committees have a role beyond that envisaged for them by the Cadbury Code, in enabling companies to acquire resources by establishing legitimacy through a demonstrable concern for reassuringly high standards of corporate governance. According to Cadbury, audit committees contribute to high standards of corporate governance: this study argues that this assertion remains unproven but that audit committees enable companies to present an image of concern about such standards which may be sufficient to establish legitimacy and access resources.

10.2 THE AUDIT COMMITTEE IN 2001

Pomeranz (1997:281) asserted that: 'It is well known that the mere act of audit committee creation is likely to have little or no effect..'

The critique of audit committees exemplified by this statement is clearly challenged by this study. From the perspective of the rhetoric embodied in the report of the committees led by Cadbury, Treadway and others, where effectiveness and criteria for its assessment are both poorly defined, audit committee creation may indeed be perceived as having 'little or no effect'[63]. However, the role of the audit committee in corporate governance has now been 'black boxed' (Callon and Latour, 1981) and is taken for granted. The demonstration of high standards of corporate governance in large UK companies has become associated in part with the existence of an audit committee which, in consequence, becomes a prerequisite for resource access: the presence or absence of an audit committee may thus have a profound effect on a company's situation, regardless of the committee's substantive activity.

Pomeranz also observed that: 'Very few studies exist which indicate any benefits, however slight, accruing from audit committee operations..' (1997:283)

He proposed that the audit committee's role should be changed 'by reintegrating it into overall board operations.'(1997:284) Does this imply that there is no task for the audit committee to undertake? This is the position of commentators such as Corrin (1993) who have argued that the full board should take responsibility for monitoring and control activity since there is no distinction in liability between NEDs and executive directors. However, recent developments in both the US and the UK have focused close attention on the audit committee and have emphasised that the audit committee is now viewed as a well-established mechanism of corporate governance.

Concerns about the integrity of financial reporting in the US and its impact on US capital markets were publicly expressed by the chairman and chief accountant of the US Securities and Exchange Commission during 1998 (Millstein 1999). In response, the New York Stock Exchange and the National Association of Securities Dealers set up the Blue Ribbon Committee on Improving the Effectiveness of Corporate Audit Committees. Rather than attempting to raise financial reporting standards by reducing areas of discretion within US GAAP (Generally Accepted Accounting Principles), the committee concentrated on the process through which this discretion is exercised and monitored 'to try to ensure that independence, awareness, diligence and care were the primary principles governing the unavoidable exercise of discretion.' (Millstein 1999:1060). The audit committee is seen as central to this process and is thus the focus of the committee's attention. The ten recommendations are intended to strengthen audit committee independence, to make audit committee operations more effective and to improve mechanisms for discussion and accountability between audit committees, external auditors and management.

Recommendations 1 and 2 set out guidelines for determining the independence of audit committee members. Recommendations 3, 4 and 5 are 'aimed at making the audit committee more effective'. Recommendation 3 requires that at least three 'financially literate' directors serve on a company's audit committee and that at least one member of the committee should have accounting or related financial management expertise. Although 'financial literacy' may seem intuitively an essential qualification for audit committee members, no evidence is cited demonstrating that lack of financial literacy has hampered audit committee effectiveness. The very few studies into the impact of members' education and experience on audit committee performance, cited in the previous section of this paper, are inconclusive in their findings. For example, DeZoort (1998) used an experimental method to examine the effect of prior experience on audit committee members' oversight judgements. He concluded that the study provided limited support for concern that lack of experience and education in certain areas might hamper audit committee members' judgement but also noted that inexperience does not 'necessarily lead to suboptimal performance' (p19). He observed: '..it is interesting to note that inexperienced members tended to be far more critical in their assessments of internal control strength…If audit committee members without experience in a relevant oversight area tend to be more critical or cautious in their approach to a problems, they may in fact be effective contributors to the overall committee effort.'(1998:17-18)

Recommendations 4 and 5 require that the audit committee adopts a detailed written charter of its responsibilities and that it should report annually to shareholders on whether it has satisfied those responsibilities. The rationale for these recommendations is based on the assumption that transparency and disclosure will boost effectiveness, but no evidence is cited in support of this. Surveys such as that conducted by Porter and Gendall (1998) suggest that clearer definition of audit committee responsibilities will improve their effectiveness but do not indicate how this may be achieved in practice. A similar 'grey area' has been noted in the context of the Cadbury recommendations by commentators such as Ezzamel and Watson (1997): '..the Cadbury Report does not spell out precisely what the new subcommittees are meant to achieve... and how, other than by simply attending meetings, the non-executives are to hold executives more

171

accountable through these new committees. This vagueness regarding purposes and means is most obvious with respect to the audit committee.' (1997:69)

Similarly, Clarke et al (1997) observed: '..the [Cadbury] code amounts to little more than a series of motherhood statements regarding the virtues directors must display and be seen to display, plus the recommendation for audit committees to be mandatory for all public companies ...... Significantly, nowhere does the code explain how the appointment of audit committees will ensure that the financial information disclosed by companies will be indicative of their wealth and progress.'(1997:239)

Once again, there is a lack of empirical research which illuminates audit committee processes against which the assumptions underpinning policy recommendations might be tested.

The remaining recommendations are designed to clarify areas of responsibility among management, external auditors and the audit committee. Recommendation 8 urges that the external auditors should discuss with the audit committee their 'judgements about the quality, not just the acceptability, of the company's accounting principles as applied in its financial reporting'. Although the concept of 'quality' in this context is not defined, guidance is given on issues to be addressed, such as 'the degree of aggressiveness or conservatism'. Recommendation 9 controversially recommends that the SEC should require audit committees to report annually to shareholders on its belief that financial statements have been prepared in accordance with GAAP. This has aroused concern about the increased burden of oversight responsibility involved and about audit committee members' liability to litigation. The report notes that similar disclosure requirements have in the past become routine and meaningless but also asserts that a formal report will raise public awareness of the audit committee's role. Again, there is no evidence cited to indicate that such reporting would increase audit committee effectiveness. The bibliography includes reports produced by professional firms and other reporting bodies but makes no reference to any academic literature, suggesting that assumptions about the relationship between disclosure and audit committee effectiveness remain untested.

In the UK, there has been less direct focus on the audit committee role within current corporate governance initiatives[64]. However, the recommendations of the Turnbull report (Turnbull 1999), which deals specifically with directors' responsibility with regard to internal control, are likely to affect audit committee activity significantly.

The Cadbury report (Cadbury Committee 1992) recommended that 'directors should make a statement in the report and accounts on the effectiveness of their system of internal control and that the auditors should report thereon' (4.32). In order to facilitate this, the report recommended that the accountancy profession should develop criteria for assessing effectiveness, together with guidance for companies on the form of such reports and guidance for auditors on procedures and the form of reports. This led to the establishment of the Rutteman working party which reported in 1994 on the basis that the Cadbury Code related to financial aspects of corporate governance and thus internal financial control, effectively limiting the apparent scope of the Cadbury requirements[65]. Subsequent corporate governance recommendations have since been consolidated into the Combined Code and compliance with this code is a requirement for listing on the London Stock Exchange. The Combined Code requires directors to maintain a sound system of internal control, financial controls forming only one element of this, and to review its effectiveness annually. Turnbull provides guidance as to how directors can meet these requirements and supersedes the Rutteman guidance.

In contrast to Cadbury, where the role of corporate governance mechanisms in controlling risk is implicit but unstated, Turnbull highlights the importance of managing risk, establishing such a close link between internal control and risk management that they appear to be almost synonymous66. This subtle semantic variation may be interpreted as reflecting a desire to reinvent internal control as risk management influenced by the aspirations of the suppliers of sophisticated risk management techniques, who are keen to ally risk management with value creation in order to sell their products. This realignment is also supported by internal auditors who are able to reinvent themselves as internal business advisors rather than monitors (Selim and McNamee 1999). This in turn echoes the shift in the broader UK corporate governance debate from a focus on financial reporting quality (Cadbury Committee 1992) to a greater concern that corporate governance mechanisms should not impede enterprise (Hampel Committee 1998), but should be viewed as instruments of value creation (Short et al, 1999).

The impact on the audit committee of the requirement to report on internal control may place an increased burden on members, particularly in companies where internal control and risk management systems are currently inadequate to meet Turnbull standards (Zaman, 2000) Alternatively, boards may wish to establish risk committees and to confine the work of the audit committee to internal financial control only. The higher profile accorded to the internal audit function, which has begun to incorporate specialists from other business areas as well as the purely financial, may lead internal auditors to press for a different reporting line, direct to the board rather than via the audit committee.

10.3   FURTHER DIRECTIONS FOR RESEARCH

There are many directions in which the methodological and theoretical approaches used here could be extended within the corporate governance framework. The use of actor-network theory to explore patterns of power and influence around boards of directors through an examination of other board subcommittees such as remuneration and strategy committees, would add significantly to the body of knowledge about boards, as advocated by writers such as Lorsch quoted in chapter 2.

In highlighting its ceremonial role, this study has suggested that the audit committee may be decoupled from the practical internal control procedures within a company: useful insight into the extent of such decoupling could be gained by using a qualitative approach to explore the relationship between the audit committee and the internal audit function more closely.

The importance of comfort generation within systems of accountability could be explored more generally using a similar approach to that of this study. Data for this study was collected in large public companies only: Conyon (1995) reported that almost 100% of FT-SE 350 companies had established audit committees by June 1995. The establishment of audit committees in smaller companies has been far more limited: Collier (1997) explored this, using a case study approach. Actor-network analysis could usefully be applied to examine how networks are formed around the boards of smaller companies and how these contribute to the demonstration of company legitimacy and access to resources.

Audit committees have been established in National Health Service Trusts and in universities (Dewing and Williams, 1995) and the Review of Audit and Accountability for Central Government (Sharman, 2001) recommended that all UK government departments should have an audit committee but very little research has yet been undertaken into their role in public sector and not-for-profit organisations. An approach similar to that used in this study could be employed to explore the development of audit committees in these institutions.

Comparative studies of audit committee activity in different countries have been undertaken (e.g. Porter and Gendall, 1993) but these have been based on surveys and published data. A qualitative approach, exploring the accounts of participants, could offer further insight into the impact of differing institutional arrangements between countries: exploring local variations in their specific context would enable the portability of corporate governance mechanisms to be assessed. Case studies based on observation and interviews, as recommended by Lorsch, would augment survey research by providing deeper insight into the dynamics of both board and audit committee behaviour within varying contexts.

Collier (1996) observed that support for audit committees by their advocates has relied on anecdotal information and concluded that 'the support for audit committees is largely based on opinions about their effectiveness and reflects an 'act of faith' rather than a decision founded on hard evidence' (1996: 124). This situation is likely to lead to unrealistic expectations about what audit committees can achieve. Further research would provide a sound underpinning for policy recommendations and could at the same time offer practical help to audit committees, bridging the gap between academic and practitioner.

10.4   CODA

'You want to know about our audit committee? Well, our deputy chairman says it's a complete waste of time because none of the members know enough about the company to make any useful contribution and they don't know what the audit committee is meant to do anyway...no, I <u>don't</u> agree with him...well, come to lunch and we'll tell you..'

One of my questions over lunch was: 'Why do you have an audit committee, then?' The answer was: 'Well, if we didn't, people would ask questions and we wouldn't look very good, would we?'

Kalbers and Fogarty referred to some of 'the deep incentives that exist in creating the façade of effectiveness in corporate governance.'

(1998:145). This study has taken a closer look at audit committee activity in an attempt to explore what happens behind that ceremonial façade.

NOTES

[1] A summary of these developments may be found in Lee, 1982, chapter 4

[2] Shleifer and Vishny (1997) provided a comprehensive review of this literature

[3] Hawley and Williams (1996) have also provided an overview of this theoretical debate

[4] Reported in <u>Corporate Governance: an International Review</u>, October 1997, 5(4), 258.

[5] SEC: Securities and Exchange Commission; NYSE: New York Stock Exchange; AICPA: American Institute of Certified Public Accountants

[6] The paper was originally published in <u>Occupational Psychology</u> (April 1952,vol. XXVI, no 2)

[7] He also expressed some sharp criticism of Cohen's use of psychological 'jargon': 'References to anal eroticism and out-groups do tend to put people off, unless they are predisposed to favour this sort of language' (Mackenzie,1953:239)

[8] Some of Wheare's comments are couched in language which echoes the famous work of Parkinson (1957). The committee as a source of humour seems to be a peculiarly British preoccupation of the post Second World War period: see also Old (1947).

[9] In the period since the interviews which form the basis of this study took place, the individuals involved have all moved to other posts, mostly with other companies, or have retired. Of the companies themselves, Runic remains largely unchanged. Scrimshaw and Hobson have undergone major reorganisations at both board and operational level and Glengarry and Harrier have disappeared through merger and divestment.

[10] Henry Morton had enquired about my training and experience and thus knew that I had worked at XYZ.

[11] The notion of comfort provision through audit committee activity is developed more fully in chapter 9.

[12] Brannen (1987) discussed this in the context of his experience as a non-participant observer at committee meetings.

[13] Explored in more detail in chapters 7 and 9.

[14] One female audit committee chair was identified in this study but it was not possible to interview her as she lives in the US and her visits to the UK are infrequent and extremely busy.

[15] There are considerable differences between audit committees in large and smaller companies and between audit committees in companies and other organisations, such as universities and NHS Trusts. This study examines large UK public companies only.

[16] This perspective links to Bailey's analysis of communication within committees discussed in section 6.3

[17] Wolcott has commented on the difficulty of separating the processes of description, analysis and interpretation of data (Wolcott,1994)

[18] The 'prophylactic' effect of the audit committee is explored in more detail in chapter 5.

[19] An extensive bibliography may be found at <http://www.comp.lancs.ac.uk/sociology/antres.html>

[20] Indeed, Callon (1987) uses the term 'simplification' rather than punctualization.

[21] It is important to understand that actor-network theory views power as an effect (part of the translation process) rather than a cause. Latour (1986) observed that 'Power over something or someone is a *composition* made by many people' but '*attributed* to one of them'

(1986:265) with the amount of power exercised varying with the number of people in the composition. Thus power is what has to be explained by the actions of the people obeying.

[22] Smith (1992) provides an overview of creative accounting techniques implicated in such scandals.

[23] There has been some resistance to the implementation of the Cadbury Code among medium-sized and smaller companies where the costs of setting up audit committees and difficulties in appointing the requisite number of NEDs have been cited as impediments: see, for example, Collier, 1997

[24] Explored in more detail in chapter 7

[25] Strongly rebutted by commentators such as Corrin (1993)

[26] Although it is not impossible that directors and auditors together may wish to test the legal and regulatory situation to provide the financial community at large with better guidance, in cases where this argument has been advanced there is usually a clear competitive advantage to the company concerned: see, for example, Power (1990, 1996)

[27] See also Beattie et al, 2001

[28] The use of the terms 'ritual' and 'ceremonial' have been extensively debated within anthropology. For example, Gluckman and Gluckman (1977) argued that 'ritual' should only be used to describe activities with a religious link. Goffman (1981:17) commented:
'The term "ritual" is not particularly satisfactory because of connotations of otherworldliness and automaticity. Gluckman's recommendation "ceremonious"... has merit except that the available nouns (ceremony and ceremonial) carry a sense of multiperson official celebration.'
Although audit committee activity is an example of 'secular ritual' (Moore and Myerhoff, 1977), the word 'ceremonial' is used in this study, following the example of Meyer and Rowan (1977). However, other writers are quoted who use the word 'ritual' in contexts where the two words could be interchangeable.

[29] Both Kunda (1992: 259) and Lukes (1975:291) noted the difficulty of interpreting ritual: Kunda concluded that '..the best one can do is to establish a plausible account that is consistent with those descriptions and native accounts one has managed to uncover.'

[30] Discussed more extensively in chapter 7

[31] Although, in the US, a small proportion of major companies do publish audit committee reports in their financial statements: see Urbancic (1996) for comment on this.

[32] See section 6.4 for a discussion of the 'passive' audit committee role.

[33] The executive directors and the external auditors can equally claim to represent shareholders' interests: mobilisation through recourse to such representative claims is illustrated in chapter 7.

[34] Statements of Standard Accounting Practice

[35] Pensions Investment Research Consultants Ltd: see <http://www.pirc.co.uk.>

[36] Lee and Stone (1997) demonstrated a gap between the potential capabilities of audit committee members as suggested by their previous experience, and the capabilities needed to fulfil audit committee responsibilities and DeZoort (1997, 1998) extended this work.

[37] Discussed in detail in chapter 7

[38] This is similar to the comment of Wheare (1955:229) that a committee must be 'wisely led and wisely fed', quoted in section 2.3.

[39] The implications of this behaviour are explored further in chapter 9.

[40] It would have been interesting to observe whether the questions had any impact on their behaviour at the next meeting.

[41] The deferential 'very tentatively' is characteristic of much of Henry's story: for such a widely respected and experienced company director, he was surprisingly self-deprecating. The possible implications of this aspect of Henry's self-presentation are discussed in section 8.2.

[42] This distinction is similar to that of Pettigrew and McNulty (1995) who distinguished between *maximalist* and *minimalist* boards.

[43] In considering the Runic stories which follow, it is important to bear in mind that, although all interviewees were asked directly about how any contentious issues were dealt with, it would not have been appropriate under the condition of confidentiality to question them in detail with reference to information revealed by a previous interviewee (although some would have liked very much to know what other interviewees had revealed - and indeed did ask). This means that the stories are inevitably incomplete, as a detailed picture of the handling of the issue was not offered by every participant involved.

[4444] SSAP 18 defines a contingency as 'a condition which exists at the balance sheet date, where the outcome will be confirmed only on the occurrence or non-occurrence of one or more uncertain future events. A contingent gain or loss is a gain or loss dependent on a contingency.' (ASC,1980, para 14). Readers should note that SSAP 18 was in force when these events took place and when they were described by interviewees, but has since been superseded by FRS 12 which redefines contingent liabilities.

[45] Power (1996) discussed the issues involved in reliance on independent professional expertise.

[46] The reason(s) why the audit committee chose to do this are not revealed. The audit committee chair does not mention this issue at all. The American NED was seen by the finance director as promoting the change in disclosure policy and the FD offered a potential explanation alluding to the NED's background. However it should be recognised that the unseen networks in which all the audit committee members have been enrolled will have considerable influence here. In this respect any ANT analysis is inevitably incomplete.

[47] Generally Accepted Accounting Principles: see Davies et al (1999)

[48] In this study the external auditor interviewed was in each case the engagement partner (see section 3.4) and is treated as a single individual , although clearly this individual represents the simplification of a powerful network, including the partners of the audit firm and their associated technical expertise and professional influence.

[49] An example of a contingent loss which had crystallised, discussed in an earlier minute

[50] A proposal to raise new finance for the company, discussed in an earlier minute.

[51] Issues arising from these individual interactions are explored further in chapter 9.

[52] The generation of comfort is explored in more detail in chapter 9.

[53] The different categorisation emphasises that the discussion which follows relates to the independence of the *audit committee* rather than the independence of the *auditor*.

[54] He provided me with a copy of his four page curriculum vitae at the beginning of the interview.

[55] However, Michael Tyler insisted that in his experience this would be very unusual and that finance directors in the Hobson group were never recruited from audit firms associated with the company.

[56] Commentators such as Porter and Gendall (1998) have cautioned against such developments, arguing that the audit committee's monitoring role would be compromised.

[57] This echoes the comments of Williams (1992) on independence as a commodity, quoted in section 8.5

[58] The subsequent issue of the Turnbull guidance for reporting on internal control is discussed in chapter 10.

[59] This seems an odd comment since consideration of the audit fee is part of the first of the duties of the audit committee listed in the specimen terms of reference in Cadbury (Cadbury Committee, 1992:73)

[60] This is inaccurate: the FRC (Financial Reporting Council) is the umbrella body which directs the policy issues associated with the UK accounting standard setting programme and does not deal with individual cases - the Financial Reporting Review Panel is the body which identifies financial reporting irregularities and may request directors to amend financial statements.

[61] Mangham (1988:83) discussed the ambivalence of membership of executive groups, the need to display differences in order that they may be resolved coupled with an awareness of the concomitant threat to group cohesion from such a display.

[62] Bourdieu, in his analysis of the generation of practices, also observed that '..conformity of practice to the rule [brings] an additional symbolic profit..' (1990:77). Bourdieu's notions of symbolic capital and profit and their generation and exchange within 'fields' parallel the exchange and market metaphors used by Collins (1981).

[63] Although there is some evidence to suggest that 'passive' audit committees established in poorly governed companies may over time develop an 'active' role which eventually raises standards (Spira, 1998).

[64] Plaistowe (1999) provided a brief comparison between the Blue Ribbon recommendations and current UK practice, noting broad similarities.

[65] Commentators such as Chambers (1997)ascribed this change to lobbying by finance directors who feared litigation

[66] See also Jones and Sutherland (1999)which couples internal control and risk management throughout

REFERENCES

Abbott, L. J., Park, Y and Parker, S., 2000. The Effects of Audit Committee Activity and Independence on Corporate Fraud. Managerial Finance 26(11), 55-67.

Accounting Standards Committee (1980) SSAP 18: Accounting for Contingencies

Alden, V.R., 1996. A firm, polite and incisive questioner. Directors & Boards. Autumn, 77.

Apostolou, B. and Strawser, J., 1990. The Role of Internal Auditor Communication with the Audit Committee. Internal Auditing, 6 (2), 35-42.

Argyris, C. and Schon, D., 1974. Theory in Practice. San Francisco: Jossey Bass.

Arora, S.L., 1988. No Tickee, No Shirtee: Proverbial Speech and Leadership in Academe. In: M.O.Jones, M.D.Moore and R.C. Snyder, eds. Inside Organizations: Understanding the Human Dimension. Newbury Park: Sage.

Arthur Andersen, 1992. Audit Committees for the 1990s. London: Arthur Andersen.

Bailey, F.G., 1965. Decisions by Consensus in Councils and Committees. In: M.Banton, ed. Political Systems and the Distribution of Power, A.S.A Monograph no.2, London: Tavistock.

Bailey, F.G., 1977. Morality and Expediency. Oxford: Blackwell

Bailey, F.G., 1983. The Tactical Uses of Passion. Ithaca: Cornell University Press.

Barber, J.D., 1966. Power in Committees: an Experiment in the Governmental Process. Chicago: Rand McNally

Bartlett, R.W., 1993. A Scale of Perceived Independence: New Evidence on an Old Concept. Accounting, Auditing and Accountability Journal. 6(2), 52-67.

Baumann, G., 1992. Ritual implicates 'Others': rereading Durkheim in a plural society. In: D. de Coppet, ed. Understanding Rituals. London: Routledge.

Baxter, W.T., 1981. Accounting Standards-Boon or Curse? Accounting and Business Research. Winter 3-10

Beasley, M. S., Carcello, J.V. and Hermanson, D.R., 1999. Audit committees: the rising expectations. Corporate Board, 20(117), 1-6.

Beasley, M. S., Carcello, J.V., Hermanson, D.R., and Lapides, P.D., 2000. Fraudulent Financial Reporting: Consideration of Industry Traits and Corporate Governance Mechanisms. Accounting Horizons 14(4), 441-454.

Beattie, V., Brandt, R. and Fearnley, S., 1996. An Empirical Study of Interaction between Auditors and Directors. Paper presented at British Accounting Association National Conference, University of Cardiff.

Beattie,V., Brandt, R. and Fearnley, S., 1997. Look to your laurels. Accountancy. July, 140-1.

Beattie, V., Fearnley, S., and Brandt, R., 2000. Behind the Audit Report: A Descriptive Study of Discussions and Negotiations Between Auditors and Directors. International Journal of Auditing 4, 177-202.

Beattie, V., Fearnley, S., and Brandt, R., 2001. Behind Closed Doors: What Company Audit is Really About. Basingstoke, Palgrave.

Berle, A.A. and Means, G.C., 1932. The Modern Corporation and Private Property. New York: Macmillan.

Bilimoria, D. and Piderit, S., 1994a. Board Committee Membership: Effects of Sex-based Bias. Academy of Management Journal, 37 (6), 1453-1477.

Bilimoria, D. and Piderit, S., 1994b. Qualifications of Corporate Board committee Members. Group and Organization Management, 19(3), 334-362.

Binder Hamlyn,1994. Non-Executive Directors – Watchdogs or Advisers? London: Binder Hamlyn.

Birkett, B.S., 1986. The Recent History of Corporate Audit Committees. The Accounting Historians Journal, 13 (2), 109-124.

Bourdieu, P., 1990. In Other Words: Essays towards a Reflexive Sociology. Cambridge: Polity Press.

Bradbury, M.E., 1990. The Incentives for Voluntary Audit Committee Formation. Journal of Accounting and Public Policy, 9 (1), 19-36.

Brannen, P., 1987. Working on directors: some methodological issues. In: G. Moyser and M. Wagstaffe, eds. Research Methods for Elite Studies. London: Allen & Unwin.

Brown, A.D., 1994. Politics, Symbolic Action and Myth Making in Pursuit of Legitimacy. Organization Studies, 15 (6), 861-878.

Cadbury Committee, 1992. Report of the Committee on the Financial Aspects of Corporate Governance. London: Gee.

Callon, M., 1986. Some elements of a sociology of translation: domestication of the scallops and the fishermen of St Brieuc Bay. In: J. Law, ed. Power, Action and Belief: a new Sociology of Knowledge? London: Routledge

Callon, M., 1987. Society in the Making: The Study of Technology as a Tool for Sociological Analysis. In: W. Bijker, T. Hughes, and T. Pinch, eds. The Social Construction of Technological Systems. Boston: MIT Press.

Callon, M. and Latour, B., 1981.Unscrewing the big Leviathan: how actors macro-structure reality and how sociologists help them to do so. In: K. Knorr-Cetina and A. Cicourel, eds. Advances in Social Theory and Methodology: towards an integration of micro- and macro-sociologies. London: Routledge and Kegan Paul.

Callon M. and Law J.,1989. On the construction of Sociotechnical Networks: Content and Context Revisited. Knowledge and Society: Studies in the Sociology of Science Past and Present, 8, 57-83.

Cameron, K.S., 1986. Effectiveness as Paradox: consensus and conflict in conceptions of organizational effectiveness. Management Science, 32 (5), 539-553.

Chambers, A., 1997. Directors' reports on internal financial control. Financial Reporting 1995/96. London, ICAEW.

Charkham, J.P., 1989. Corporate governance and the market for control of companies. London: Bank of England.

Charkham, J.P., 1995. Keeping Good Company: a Study of Corporate Governance in Five Countries. Oxford: Oxford University Press.

Chua W.F., 1995. Experts, Networks and Inscriptions in the Fabrication of Accounting Images: a story of the representation of three public hospitals. Accounting, Organizations and Society, 20(2/3),111-145.

Clarke F., Dean G., Oliver K., 1997. Corporate Collapse: Regulatory, Accounting and Ethical Failure. Melbourne: Cambridge University Press.

Cobb, L., 1993. An investigation into the effect of selected audit committee characteristics on fraudulent financial reporting . Doctoral dissertation, University of South Florida.

Cochran, P. and Wartick, S., 1988. Corporate Governance: a Review of the Literature. Financial Executives Research Foundation.

Cohen, J., 1952. Study of Committees and Conferences. Public Administration, xxx, Winter, 361-367.

Collier, P.,1992. Audit Committees in Large UK Companies. London: ICAEW.

Collier, P., 1993. Audit Committees in Major UK Companies. Managerial Auditing Journal, 8 (3), 25-30.

Collier, P., 1996. The rise of the audit committee in UK quoted companies: a curious phenomenon? Accounting, Business and Financial History, 6 (2), 121-140.

Collier, P.,1997. Audit Committees in Smaller Listed Companies. In: K. Keasey and M. Wright, eds. Corporate Governance: Responsibilities, Risks and Remuneration Chichester: John Wiley.

Collier, P. and Gregory, A., 1996. Audit Committee Effectiveness and the Audit Fee. European Accounting Journal, 5 (2), 177-199.

Collins H. and Yearley, S., 1992. Epistemological Chicken. In: A. Pickering, ed. Science as Practice and Culture. Illinois: University of Chicago.

Collins, R., 1981. On the Microfoundations of Macrosociology. American Journal of Sociology 86(5), 984-1014.

Conyon, M., 1995. Cadbury in the Boardroom. The Corporate Register Hemmington Scott. June, 5-10.

Coombes, P. and Watson, M., 2000. Three surveys on corporate governance. The McKinsey Quarterly, 4, 74-77.

Cornford, F.M., 1953. Microcosmographia Academica, Cambridge: Heffer.

Corrin, J., 1993. A blatant slur on executive directors' integrity. Accountancy, April, 81.

Czarniawska-Joerges, B., 1992. Exploring Complex Organizations: a Cultural Perspective. Newbury Park: Sage.

Daily, C and Dalton, D., 2001. Corporate Governance Digest. Business Horizons, March/April, 3-6

Davies, M., Paterson R. and Wilson, A., 1999. UK GAAP: Generally Accepted Accounting Practice in the United Kingdom. 6th ed. London: Ernst and Young/Macmillan.

Davis, G.F. and Thompson, J.A., 1994. A Social Movement Perspective on Corporate Control. Administrative Science Quarterly, 39, 141-173.

Davis, S.,1997. Leading Corporate Governance Indicators. In: Governance, 53, October, 10.

Deakin, S. and Hughes, A., 1997. Comparative Corporate Governance: an Interdisciplinary Agenda. Journal of Law and Society, 24 (1), 1-9.

Deloitte and Touche, 1996. Avoiding Corporate Governance Overload. London: Deloitte and Touche.

Demb, A. and Neubauer, F., 1992. The Corporate Board: Confronting the Paradoxes. Oxford: Oxford University Press.

Dewing, I.P. and Williams, B.C., 1995. The role of audit committees in UK universities. Managerial Auditing Journal. 10 (6), 10-16.

DeZoort, F.T., 1997. An Investigation of Audit Committees' Oversight Responsibilities. Abacus, 33 (2), 208-227.

DeZoort, F.T., 1998. An Analysis of Experience Effects on Audit Committee Members' Oversight Judgements. Accounting, Organizations and Society. 23 (1), 1-21

Dimaggio, P.J and Powell, W.W., 1983. The Iron Cage Revisited: Institutional Isomorphism and Collective Rationality in Organizational Fields. American Sociological Review, 48, 147-160.

Donaldson, L., 1990. The Ethereal Hand: Organizational Economics and Management Theory. Academy of Management Review. 15(3), 369-381

Ecton W. and Reinstein R., 1982. Audit Committees: can they be more effective? Financial Executive, November, 32-37.

Eichenseher, J.W. and Shields, D., 1985. Corporate Director Liability and Monitoring Preferences. Journal of Accounting and Public Policy, 4 (1), 13-31.

Ezzamel, M.,1994. Organizational Change and Accounting: Understanding the Budgeting system in its Organizational Context. Organization Studies, 15(1), 213-40

Ezzamel, M. and Watson, R.,1997. Wearing Two Hats: The Conflicting Control and Management roles of Non-Executive Directors. In: K.Keasey, S. Thompson and M. Wright, eds. Corporate Governance: Economic, Management and Financial Issues. Oxford: Oxford University Press

Falk, H. and Frucot, V., 1997. Perceived Auditor Independence. Asia-Pacific Journal of Accounting, 4(1), 94-107.

183

Feldman, M.S. and March J.G., 1981. Information in Organizations as Sign and Symbol. Administrative Science Quarterly, 26, 171-186.

Felton, R., Hudnut, A. and van Heeckeren, J.,1996. Putting a value on board governance. McKinsey Quarterly, 4, 170.

Finch, V.,1992. Company Directors: Who Cares about Skill and Care? Modern Law Review.55(2), 179-214.

Forker, J.J., 1992. Corporate Governance and Disclosure Quality. Accounting and Business Research, 22 (86), 111-124.

Gersick, C.J. and Hackman, R., 1990. Habitual Routines in Task Performing. Organizational Behaviour and Human Decision Processes, 47, 65-97.

Glaser, B. and Strauss, A., 1967. The Discovery of Grounded Theory: Strategies of Qualitative Research. New York: Aldine.

Gluckman, M, and Gluckman, M., 1977. On Drama and Games and Athletic Contests. In: S.F. Moore and B.G. Myerhoff, eds. Secular Ritual, Assen/Amsterdam: Van Gorcum.

Goffman, E., 1981. Forms of Talk. Oxford: Basil Blackwell.

Greenbury, R.,1995. Directors' Remuneration: Report of a Study Group Chaired by Sir Richard Greenbury. London: Gee.

Griffiths, I., 1995. New Creative Accounting. London: Macmillan.

Grout, P., Jewitt, I., Pong, C. and Whittington, G., 1994. 'Auditor professional judgement': implications for regulation and the law. Economic Policy, October, 309-350

Guthrie, J. and Turnbull, S.,1995. Audit Committees: Is there a role for Corporate Senates and/or Stakeholders Councils? Corporate Governance: an International Review, 3 (2), 78-89.

Gwilliam, D., 1987. A Survey of Auditing Research. London: ICAEW

Hampel Committee, 1998. Committee on Corporate Governance, Final Report. London: Gee.

Harvey, J.B., 1988. The Abilene paradox: the management of agreement. Organizational Dynamics, 17(1), 17-34.

Harré, R. and Secord, P.F., 1972. The Explanation of Social Behaviour. Oxford: Basil Blackwell.

Harrison, J.R., 1987. The Strategic Use of Board Committees. California Management Review, 30 (1), 109-125.

Hawley, J.P. and Williams, A.T., 1996. Corporate Governance in the United States: the Rise of Fiduciary Capitalism. Working paper, St Mary's College of California.

Herzel, L., 1990. Corporate Governance through Statistical Eyes. Journal of Financial Economics, 27, 581-593.

Hilmer, F.G., 1993. Strictly Boardroom: the report of an Independent Working Party into Corporate Governance. Information Australia, Melbourne and the Sydney Institute, Sydney.

Holstein, J.A. and Gubrium, J.F., 1997. Active Interviewing. In: D. Silverman, ed. Qualitative Research: Theory, Method and Practice. London: Sage.

Humphrey, C., 1997. Debating Audit Expectations. In: M. Sherer and S. Turley, ed. Current Issues in Auditing. London: Paul Chapman Publishing Ltd.

Hussey, J. and Hussey, R. 1997. Business Research. London: Macmillan

Hussey, R. and Jack A., 1995. The Finance Director and the Auditor. Bristol: University of the West of England.

Institute of Chartered Accountants in England and Wales (ICAEW),1994. Non Executive Directorship: a Guide for Chartered Accountants. London: ICAEW.

Institute of Chartered Accountants in England and Wales (ICAEW),1996. Corporate Governance: Developing a Charter for Success. London: ICAEW.

Institute of Chartered Accountants in England and Wales (ICAEW),1997a. Audit Committees: a Framework for Assessment. London: ICAEW.

Institute of Chartered Accountants in England and Wales (ICAEW),1997b. Members Handbook, 1.201,181-199.

Institute of Chartered Accountants in England and Wales (ICAEW), 2001. The Effective Audit committee: a challenging role. London: ICAEW.

Janis, I.L., 1985. Sources of error in strategic decision-making. In: J.M. Pennings et al, eds. Organizational Strategy and Change. San Francisco: Jossey Bass.

Jensen, M.C. and Meckling, W.H.,1976. Theory of the Firm: Managerial Behaviour, Agency Costs and Ownership Structure. Journal of Financial Economics, 3, 305-360.

Johnson, J.L, Daily C.M. and Ellstrand, A.E., 1996. Boards of directors: a review and research agenda. Journal of Management. 22 (3), 409-439

Jonas, G. and Blanchet, J., 2000. Assessing Quality of Financial Reporting. Accounting Horizons 14(3), 353-363.

Jones, M., 1996. Corporate Governance Disclosure. London: Deloitte Touche Tohmatsu International.

Jones, M. and Sutherland, G., 1999. Implementing Turnbull: A Boardroom Briefing. London, ICAEW.

Kalbers L., 1992. An Examination of the Relationship between Audit Committees and External Auditors. Ohio CPA Journal. December, 19-27.

Kalbers L. and Fogarty T., 1993. Audit Committee Effectiveness: an Empirical Investigation of the Contribution of Power. Auditing: a Journal of Practice and Theory, 12 (1), 24-49

Kalbers, L. P. and T. J. Fogarty (1998). Organizational and Economic Explanations of Audit Committee Oversight. Journal of Managerial Issues , X(2), 129-150.

Kay, J., 1996. The Business of Economics. Oxford: Oxford University Press.

Institute of Chartered Accountants of Scotland (ICAS),1988. Making Corporate Reports Valuable. London: Kogan Page.

Keasey, K. and Wright, M., 1993. Issues in Corporate Accountability and Governance: an Editorial. Accounting and Business Research, 23 (91A), 291-303.

Keasey, K. and Wright, M., 1997. Corporate Governance, Accountability and Enterprise. In: K. Keasey and M. Wright, eds. Corporate Governance: Responsibilities, Risks and Remuneration. Chichester: John Wiley and Sons

Keasey, K., Thompson, S. and Wright, M.,1997. Introduction. In: K.Keasey, S. Thompson and M. Wright, eds. Corporate Governance: Economic, Management and Financial Issues. Oxford: Oxford University Press.

Knapp, M., 1987. An Empirical Study of Audit Committee Support for Auditors Involved in Technical Disputes with Client Management. The Accounting Review, LXII (3), 578-588.

Kochan, N and Syrett, M., 1991. New Directions in Corporate Governance. London: Business International Ltd.

Kunda, G., 1992. Engineering Culture: control and commitment in a high-tech corporation. Philadelphia: Temple University Press.

Latour, B.,1986. The powers of association. In: J.Law, ed. Power, Action and Belief: a new Sociology of Knowledge? London: Routledge.

Law, J.,1992. Notes on the Theory of the Actor-Network: Ordering, Strategy and Heterogeneity. Systems Practice, 5(4), 379-393.

Law, J. and Callon, M., 1992. The life and death of an aircraft: a network analysis of technical change. In: W.E Bijker and J. Law, eds. 'Shaping Technology - Building Society'. Boston: MIT Press.

Law, J.,1997. Traduction/Trahison – Notes on ANT. Centre for Social Theory and Technology, Keele University at:http://www.comp.lancs.ac.uk/sociology/antres.html

Lee, N. and Brown, S., 1994. Otherness and the Actor Network: the Undiscovered Continent. American Behavioural Scientist, 37(6), 772-790.

Lee, T.A., 1982. Company Financial Reporting. 2nd ed. Wokingham: Van Nostrand Rheinhold.

185

Lee, T. and Stone, M., 1997. Economic Agency and Audit Committees: Responsibilities and Membership Composition. International Journal of Auditing, 1(2), 97-116.

Lindsell, D., 1992. Blueprint for an Effective Audit Committee. Accountancy, December, 104.

Lorsch, J.W and MacIver, E., 1989. Pawns or Potentates: The Reality of America's Corporate Boards. Boston: Harvard Business School Press.

Lukes, S., 1975. Political Ritual and Social Integration. Sociology, 9, 289-308.

Mace, M., 1971. Directors: Myth and Reality. Boston: Harvard University Press

Mackenzie, W.J.M., 1953. Committees in Administration. Public Administration, xxxi, 235-244.

Maddick H. and Pritchard E.P.,1958. The Conventions of Local Authorities in the West Midlands: Part I . Public Administration, Summer,145-155

Maddick H and Pritchard E.P., 1959. The Conventions of Local Authorities in the West Midlands: Part II. Public Administration, Summer, 135-143

Mangham, I.L., 1986. Power and Performance in Organizations: an Exploration of Executive Process. Oxford: Basil Blackwell.

Mangham, I.L., 1988. Effecting Organizational change: Further Explorations of the Executive Process. Oxford: Basil Blackwell.

Mangham, I.L. and Pye, A., 1991. The Doing of Managing. Oxford: Blackwell.

Marrian, I., 1988. Audit Committees. Edinburgh: Institute of Chartered Accountants in Scotland

Mautz, R.K and Neumann, F.L., 1970. Corporate Audit Committees. Urbana: University of Illinois.

May, T., 1997. Social Research: issues, methods and process. 2nd ed. Buckingham: Open University Press.

Mayer, C., 1997. Corporate Governance, Competition and Performance. Journal of Law and Society, 24 (1), 152-176.

McMullen, D.A., 1996. Audit Committee Performance: An Investigation of the Consequences Associated with Audit Committees. Auditing: a Journal of Practice and Theory. 15 (1), 87-103.

McMullen, D. A. and Raghunandan, K., 1996. Enhancing Audit Committee Effectiveness. Journal of Accountancy , 182(2), 79-81.

Menon, K. and Williams, J., 1994. The Use of Audit Committees for Monitoring. Journal of Accounting and Public Policy, 13, 121-139.

Meyer, J.W. and Rowan, B., 1977. Institutionalized Organizations; formal Structure as Myth and Ceremony. American Journal of Sociology, 83 (2), 340-363.

Michael, M., 1996. Constructing Identities. London: Sage.

Mills, C. W.,1940. Situated Actions and Vocabularies of Motive. American Sociological Review, 5, 904-913.

Millstein, I. M. (1999). Introduction to the Report and Recommendations of the Blue Ribbon Committee on Improving the Effectiveness of Corporate Audit Committees. Business Lawyer , 54(3), 1057-1066.

Moore, S.F. and Myerhoff, B.G., eds., 1977. Secular Ritual, Assen/Amsterdam: Van Gorcum.

Muth, M.M. and Donaldson, L., 1998. Stewardship Theory and board Structure: a contingency approach. Corporate Governance; an International Review. 6 (1), 5-28.

Myerhoff, B.G., 1977. We Don't Wrap Herring in a Printed Page: Fusion, Fictions and Continuity in Secular Ritual. In: S.F. Moore and B.G. Myerhoff, eds., Secular Ritual, Assen/Amsterdam: Van Gorcum.

Neal, S.,1995. Researching Powerful People from a Feminist and Racist Perspective: a note on gender, collusion and marginality. British Educational Research Journal, 21 (4), 517-531.

Old, B., 1946. On the Mathematics of Committees, Boards and Panels. The Scientific Monthly,63, 129-134

O'Sullivan, M. (2000). Contests for Corporate Control: Corporate Governance and Economic Performance in the United States and Germany. Oxford, Oxford University Press.

Oxford Analytica Ltd., 1992. Board Directors and Corporate Governance: trends in the G7 countries over the next ten years. Oxford: Oxford Analytica Ltd.

Page, M., 1991. Now is the time to be more critical. Accountancy, October, 31.

Page, M., 1992. Turn again, Professor Whittington. Accountancy, February, 30.

Pahl, R.E. and Winkler, J.J.,1974. The Economic Elite: theory and practice. In: P. Stanworth and A. Giddens, eds. Elites and Power in British Society . Cambridge: Cambridge University Press.

Parker, L.D. and Roffey, B. H., 1997. Back to the drawing board: revisiting grounded theory and the everyday accountant's and manager's reality. Accounting, Auditing and Accountability Journal, 10 (2), 212-247.

Parkinson, C. Northcote., 1957. Parkinson's Law. London: John Murray.

Peat Marwick McLintock, 1987. The Audit Committee. London: Peat Marwick McLintock.

Pentland, B.,1993. Getting Comfortable with the Numbers: Auditing and the Micro-production of Macro-order. Accounting, Organizations and Society, 18(7/8), 605-620.

Pettigrew, A.M.,1992. On Studying Managerial Elites. Strategic Management Journal, 13, 163-182.

Pettigrew, A.M. and McNulty, T., 1995. Power and Influence in and around the Boardroom. Human Relations, 48 (8), 845-874.

Pfeffer, J., 1972. Size and Composition of Corporate Boards of Directors: the Organization and its Environment. Administrative Science Quarterly, 17, 218-228

Pimm, D.A., 1994. Corporate Governance Disclosures. In: D.J. Tonkin and L.C. Skerratt, eds. Financial Reporting 1992-93 . London: ICAEW.

Plaistowe, I., 1999. The US and the UK. Accountancy , April, 113.

Pomeranz, F., 1997. Audit committees: where do we go from here? Managerial Auditing Journal, 12 (6), 281-284.

Pound, J., 1992. Beyond Takeovers: Politics Comes to Corporate Control. Harvard Business Review, March-April, 83-93.

Pound, J., 1993. The Rise of the Political Model of Corporate Governance and Corporate Control. New York University Law Review, 68 (5), 1003-1071.

Porter, B. and Gendall, P., 1993. An International Comparison of the Development and Role of Audit Committees in the Private Corporate Sector. Paper presented at European Accounting Association Conference, Turku, Finland

Porter, B. A. and P. J. Gendall (1998). Audit committees in Private and Public Sector Corporates in New Zealand: An Empirical Investigation. International Journal of Auditing , 2, 49-69.

Power, M.,ed.,1990. Brand and Goodwill Accounting Strategies. Cambridge: Woodhead-Faulkner.

Power, M., 1996. Making Things Auditable. Accounting, Organizations and Society. 21 (2/3), 289-315.

Power, M., 1997. The Audit Society: Rituals of Verification. Oxford: Oxford University Press.

Price Waterhouse/Institute of Internal Auditors Research Foundation,1993. Improving Audit Committee Performance :What Works Best. PW/IIARF.

PricewaterhouseCoopers, 2001. Non-Executive Directors: A survey of practice and opinion. London, PricewaterhouseCoopers.

PRONED, 1993. Audit Committees. London: PRONED.

Puwar, N., 1997. Reflections on Interviewing Women MPs. Sociological Research Online,2(1), http://www.socresonline.org.uk/socresonline/2/1/4.html

Pye, A., (2001). Corporate Boards, Investors and their Relationships: accounts of accountability and corporate governing in action. Corporate Governance: An International Review, 9(3), 186-195.

Raghunandan, K. and McHugh, J.A., 1994. Internal Auditors' Independence and Interactions with Audit Committees: Challenges of Form and Substance. Advances in Accounting, 12, 313-333.

Raghunandan, K., Read, W.J., and Rama, D.V., 2001. Audit Committee Composition, 'Grey Directors,' and Interaction with Internal Auditing. Accounting Horizons 15(2), 105-119.

Rezaee, Z. and Lander, G.H., 1993. The Internal Auditor's Relationship with the Audit Committee. Managerial Auditing Journal, 8 (3), 35-40.

Robson, K.,1991. On the Arenas of Accounting Change: the Process of Translation. Accounting, Organizations and Society. 16 (5/6), 547-570.

Samet, J.I. and Sherman, J.A., 1984. The audit committee: in search of a purpose. Corporation Law Review, 7 (1), 42-55.

Samuels, J.M, Greenfield, S and Piper, A., 1996. The role of non-executive directors post-Cadbury. Journal of General Management, 21 (4), 1-14.

Sharman, C., 2001. Holding to Account: the Review of Audit and Accountability for Central Government. London.

Schneider, A and Wilner, N., 1990. A Test of Audit Deterrent to Financial Reporting Irregularities. Accounting Review, 65 (3), 668-681.

Schwartzman, H.B., 1989. The Meeting: Gatherings in Organizations and Communities. New York: Plenum.

Selim, G. and McNamee, D., 1999. Risk Management and Internal Auditing: What are the Essential Building Blocks for a Successful Paradigm Change?" International Journal of Auditing 3(2), 147-155.

Shleifer, A. and Vishny, R.,1997. A Survey of Corporate Governance. The Journal of Finance, LII (2), 737-83.

Short, H., Keasey, K., Wright, M. and Hull, A.,1999. Corporate governance: from accountability to enterprise. Accounting and Business Research 29(4), 337-352.

Sillince, J. (2000). Rhetorical power, accountability and conflict in committees: an argumentation approach. Journal of Management Studies, 37(8), 1125-1156.

Silverman, D.,1993. Interpreting Qualitative Data: Methods for Analysing Talk, Text and Interaction. London: Sage.

Singleton, V. and Michael, M., 1993. Actor-Networks and Ambivalence: General Practitioners in the UK Cervical Screening Programme. Social Studies of Science, 23, 227-64.

Smith, A.,1976. An Inquiry into the Nature and Causes of The Wealth of Nations. Oxford: Clarendon Press.

Smith, T.,1992. Accounting for Growth. London: Century Business.

Sommer, A., 1991. Auditing Audit Committees: an Educational Opportunity for Auditors. Accounting Horizons. June, 91-93.

Spangler, W.D. and Braiotta, L., 1990. Leadership and Corporate Audit Committee Effectiveness. Group and Organization Studies, 15 (2), 134-157.

Spencer, A., 1983. On the Edge of the Organization: the Role of the Outside Director. Chichester: John Wiley.

Spira, L.F., 1995. The Audit Committee: Pawn or Panacea?' Journal of Applied Accounting Research, 2 (III), 64-88.

Spira, L.F., 1997a. They don't work, they can't work, they shouldn't work: some perspectives on audit committees. Paper presented at the Financial Reporting and Communication Conference, Cardiff Business School, July

188

Spira, L.F., 1997b. The Comforting Role of the Audit Committee .Paper presented at British Accounting Association South East Area Regional Conference, Nene College of Higher Education, September

Spira, L.F.,1998. An Evolutionary Perspective on Audit Committee Effectiveness. Corporate Governance: an International Review, 6(1), 29-38.

Spira, L. F., 1999a. Ceremonies of governance: perspectives on the role of the audit committee. Journal of Management and Governance 3(3), 231-260.

Spira, L. F., 1999b. Independence in Corporate Governance: the Audit Committee Role. Business Ethics: a European Review 8(4), 262-273.

Stiles, P., 2001. The impact of the board on strategy: an empirical examination. Journal of Management Studies ,38(5), 627-650.

Strauss, A. and Corbin, J.,1990. Basics of Qualitative Research: Grounded Theory Procedure and Techniques. Newbury Park: Sage.

Teoh, H.Y. and Lim, C.C., 1996. An Empirical Study of the Effects of Audit Committees, Disclosure of Nonaudit Fees and Other Issues on Audit Independence: Malaysian Evidence. Journal of International Accounting, Auditing and Taxation, 5 (2), 231-248.

Treadway Commission, 1987. Report of the National Commission on Fraudulent Financial Reporting.

Tricker, R., 1978. The Independent Director: a study of the non-executive director and the audit committee. London:Tolley

Tricker, R., 1993. Editorial. Corporate Governance: an International Review, 1(1),1-4.

Tricker R., 1994. Editorial. Corporate Governance: an International Review, 2(2), 56

Tricker, R., 1996. Corporate Governance: the Ideological Imperative. In: H. Thomas and D. O'Neal, eds. Strategic Integration. Chichester: Wiley.

Tsui J., Subramanian N. and Hoy, S., 1994. The Effects of Audit Committees on Bankers' Perceptions of Auditor Independence. Corporate Governance: an International Review, 2(2), 101-107 .

Tuckman, B., 1965. Developmental Sequence in Small Groups. Psychological Bulletin, 63(6), 384-99.

Turnbull, S., 1994. Competitiveness and Corporate Governance. Corporate Governance: an International Review. 2(2), 80-86.

Turnbull Committee, 1999. Internal control: Guidance for Directors on the Combined Code. London, ICAEW.

Urbancic, F., 1996. A Content Analysis of Audit Committee Reports. Internal Auditing, Summer, 36-42.

Verschoor,C.C., 1990a. MiniScribe: a new example of audit committee ineffectiveness. Internal Auditing , 5(4), 13-19

Verschoor, C.C., 1990b. The Aftermath of Audit Committee Ineffectiveness at Miniscribe. Internal Auditing, 5(5), 25-28.

Wallman, S.M.H., 1996. The Future of Accounting, Part III: Reliability and Auditor Independence. Accounting Horizons, 10(4), 76-97.

Warrick, W.W. and Galloway D.J., 1996. The Governance Audit: How can we make sure we don't get surprised? Directorship, XXII (5).

Wheare, K.C., 1955. Government by Committee. Oxford: Clarendon Press.

Whittington, G., 1991. Good stewardship and the ASB's objectives. Accountancy, November, 33.

Wild, J.J, 1994. Managerial Accountability to Shareholders: Audit Committees and the Explanatory Power of Earnings for Returns. British Accounting Review. 26(4), 353-374.

Wild, J.J, 1996. The audit committee and earnings quality. Journal of Accounting, Auditing and Finance, 11 (2), 247-76.

Williams, P.F., 1992. Prediction and Control in Accounting 'Science'. Critical Perspectives on Accounting, 3(1), 99-107.

Winkler, J., 1987. The fly on the wall of the inner sanctum: observing company directors at work. In: G. Moyser and M. Wagstaffe, eds. Research Methods for Elite Studies. London: Allen & Unwin.

Wolcott, H.,1994. Transforming Qualitative Data: Description, Analysis and Interpretation. Thousand Oaks: Sage.

Wolnizer, P.W., 1987. Auditing as Independent Authentication. Sydney: Sydney University Press.

Wolnizer, P.W., 1995. Are Audit Committees Red Herrings? Abacus, 31 (1), 45-66.

Yonay, Y.P., 1994. When Black Boxes Clash: Competing Ideas of What Science Is in Economics, 1924-39. Social Studies of Science, 24, 39-80.

Zahra, S.A. and Pearce, J.A.,1989. Boards of Directors and Corporate Financial Performance. Journal of Management, 15 (2), 291-334.

Zaman, M., 2000. Turnbull - generating undue expectations of the corporate governance role of audit committees. Managerial Auditing Journal 15(4), 149-152.

190

INDEX

acronyms.................... 101
actor-network theory
    explanation........................... 55
    translation....................... 58, 74
agency theory 10, 11, 13, 14
audit committee
    agenda 89
    as deterrent........................... 78
    as network 82
    ceremonial...... 69, 81, 157, 165
    criticism of............................ 6
    definition........................... 1, 5
    development........................ 169
    effectiveness.............. 7, 20, 133
    evolution 104
    literature.............................. 15
    meetings.............................. 89
    minutes.......................... 89, 93
    participants.................... 43, 119
    purpose................................ 16
    relationships........................ 26
    role 5
audit committee meetings
    numbers attending............... 96
    place................................... 95
    seating arrangements.......... 102
    timing................................. 97
Blue Ribbon Committee... 22, 170
boards of directors
    access 42, 47
    literature.............................. 12
    studies of............................. 13

Cadbury Committee...5, 18, 65, 73,
    108, 120, 123, 173
comfort
    as a commodity........... 147, 159
    in auditing........................... 147
committees
    literature 26
consensus................................124
contentious issues....................109
contingencies 113
conventions of behaviour........100
corporate governance
    definition 3
    international......................4, 10
    literature 9, 15
    models 11
    premium 74, 161
external auditors 75, 120, 139
Greenbury Committee 47, 66
Hampel Committee............21, 66
independence 127
    as a commodity...................144
    auditor 120, 128
    of non-executive directors128,
    130
institutional isomorphism.......162
internal audit..........................151
internal control.......................151
legitimacy 161
stakeholder theory....................14
stewardship theory..............4, 14
Treadway Commission.............66
Turnbull report.......................172